FROM THE BIBLE-TEACHING MINISTRY OF
CHARLES R. SWINDOLL

FAMOUS
LAST WORDS

Last words are often significant words. They give perspective to life and reveal what's truly important. With their last few breaths, those whose time on earth has come to an end may share what their lifetime has taught them. Some words are inspiring. Some are tragic. All are valuable.

If you would like to gain a fresh, biblical perspective to carry you through life, then this resource is for you! Delve into the last words of both familiar and unfamiliar people in the Bible with *Famous Last Words*. This devotional includes:

- A discussion of the last words of twenty-two selected characters from the Old and New Testaments
- An opportunity to learn from the successes and failures of people just like you
- Encouraging application points for your life today

It's time to discover the famous last words of Athaliah, Agag, Samson, Simeon, Joseph, Jesus, and others! Their dying words will inspire you to truly live.

CHAPTER : VERSE

FAMOUS LAST WORDS
Living with the End in Mind

From the Bible-Teaching Ministry of Charles R. Swindoll

Charles R. Swindoll has devoted his life to the accurate, practical teaching and application of God's Word and His grace. A pastor at heart, Chuck has served as senior pastor to congregations in Texas, Massachusetts, and California. Since 1998, he has served as the founder and senior pastor-teacher of Stonebriar Community Church in Frisco, Texas, but Chuck's listening audience extends far beyond a local church body. As a leading program in Christian broadcasting since 1979, *Insight for Living* airs in major Christian radio markets around the world, reaching people groups in languages they can understand. Chuck's extensive writing ministry has also served the body of Christ worldwide and his leadership as president and now chancellor of Dallas Theological Seminary has helped prepare and equip a new generation for ministry. Chuck and Cynthia, his partner in life and ministry, have four grown children, ten grandchildren, and two great-grandchildren.

Published By
IFL Publishing House
A Division of Insight for Living Ministries
Post Office Box 1050
Frisco, Texas 75034-0018

Editor in Chief: Cynthia Swindoll, President, Insight for Living Ministries
Executive Vice President: Wayne Stiles, Th.M., D.Min., Dallas Theological Seminary
Writers: John Adair, Th.M., Ph.D., Dallas Theological Seminary
Jim Craft, M.A., English, Mississippi College
Malia Rodriguez, Th.M., Dallas Theological Seminary
Wayne Stiles, Th.M., D.Min., Dallas Theological Seminary
Content Editor: Amy L. Snedaker, B.A., English, Rhodes College
Copy Editors: Jim Craft, M.A., English, Mississippi College
Paula McCoy, B.A., English, Texas A&M University-Commerce
Project Coordinator, Creative Ministries: Megan Meckstroth, B.S., Advertising, University of Florida
Project Coordinator, Publishing: Melissa Cleghorn, B.A., University of North Texas
Proofreader: Paula McCoy, B.A., English, Texas A&M University-Commerce
Designer: Margaret Gulliford, B.A., Graphic Design, Taylor University
Production Artist: Nancy Gustine, B.F.A., Advertising Art, University of North Texas

ISBN: 978-1-62655-003-2
Printed in the United States of America

TABLE OF CONTENTS

CHAPTER:VERSE

A LETTER FROM CHUCK

L ast words are often great words. As people reach the end of the trail, their final words can give us amazing perspective on the pressures of the present, the worries of the past, or even our fears of the future. There's something great about wrapping up life in a few words, which probably explains the reason we lean over and listen closely to dying words.

If you visit the gravesite of Martin Luther King, Jr. in Atlanta, you will see three words that beautifully encompass King's life and work: "Free at last . . ." Toward the end of the Great War—as World War I was called—Winston Churchill said that three words would best fit those white crosses and stars of David that dot the landscape and battle-grounds at home and abroad: "Not in vain . . ."

After Abraham Lincoln had been assassinated, several close friends surrounded

Lincoln's body. One of his cabinet members, upon hearing the physician's pronouncement of death, put his hat over his heart and said, "And now he belongs to the ages."

While searching for a title for the seventy-fifth chapter of his four-volume work on Lincoln, *The War Years*, Carl Sandburg chose a title from an old woodsman's proverb. Only eight eloquent words encapsulate the significance of life: "A tree is best measured when it's down."

I don't know if you've stopped to think about it, but there are epitaphs and last words woven throughout the Scriptures. They appear like eloquent landmarks of lives. Enoch's epitaph was brief: "God took him" (Genesis 5:24). King Uzziah made a miserable mess of the latter part of his life, leaving people to speak these simple words about him: "He is a leper" (2 Chronicles 26:23). Paul chose his own epitaph, portraying his life in just a few words: "I have fought the good fight. I have finished the course. I have kept the faith" (2 Timothy 4:7). That says it all, doesn't it? Last words are like that.

Last words matter because they do several things. Last words clarify. They blow the fog away and clarify what this life has been about. Last words solidify. They take you away from the murky, sandy soil of opinions and ideas and solidify life in just a few words. Last words prioritize. They communicate what our priorities should be in this life. Last words also summarize. They tell us something of what life's all about.

In *Famous Last Words*, we've collected and written about the last words of some notable people in the Bible. Some you'll have heard of — Moses, David, and Jesus. Others might be new to you — Athaliah, Agag, and Sapphira. Each devotional will help you measure the lives of these biblical figures. Will you do me a favor? As you measure these biblical lives, take your own life-measurements as well. Are you where you want to be with the Lord? I hope that this book will help you mark the way toward a life of vibrant faith and selfless action.

Charles R. Swindoll

Charles R. Swindoll

FAMOUS
LAST WORDS

CHAPTER : VERSE

ISAAC'S BLESSING

"Now may God give you of the dew of heaven, And of the fatness of the earth, And an abundance of grain and new wine; May peoples serve you, And nations bow down to you; Be master of your brothers, And may your mother's sons bow down to you. Cursed be those who curse you, And blessed be those who bless you."
—*Genesis 27:28–29*

Isaac lived a long life and witnessed God's faithfulness. Born as a result of a miraculous conception in his parents' old age and raised by Abraham, the righteous man who was called God's friend (James 2:23), Isaac had a blessed childhood. Isaac saw his father's trust in the Lord when Abraham took Isaac up to Mount Moriah to sacrifice him to God (Genesis 22:3). Isaac experienced God's deliverance when God provided, instead, a ram for the offering (22:13–14). And Isaac heard the angel of the Lord reaffirm God's covenant with Abraham to bless Abraham's people, to make them as numerous as the stars in heaven, and to bless all people through Abraham's seed (22:15–18). As a boy, Isaac witnessed the importance of God's blessing.

After Isaac married Rebekah, they took their boys, Jacob and Esau, to Gerar in the land of the Philistines to find food during the famine. While they were in Gerar, the Lord spoke to Isaac and extended to him the Abrahamic covenant. God promised to bless Isaac, to give him the land in which he was living, to multiply his descendants, and to bless all the nations of the earth through his people (Genesis 26:2–5). As a man, Isaac received God's blessing.

In addition to being blessed personally, Isaac understood the importance of the blessing to his family—especially since his family blessing came straight from the Lord. Abraham's blessing pointed to his favored status with God and also carried the expectation that Abraham would live an obedient life appropriate to his calling. After God extended Abraham's blessing to Isaac, Isaac knew he would have to live in a way that reflected God's blessing on his life. And since God's covenant with Abraham included a blessing on Abraham's descendants, Isaac

was to pass on this blessing to the next generation.

So, as the elderly Isaac faced imminent death, he called for his firstborn son, Esau, to whom he would pass the family blessing. But Isaac had neglected God's command. Many years earlier, God had told Rebekah that, even though the social convention was to bless the oldest son, their older son would serve their younger son. Jacob was to get the blessing, not Esau (25:23).

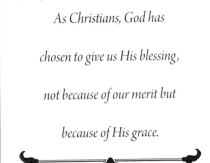

As Christians, God has chosen to give us His blessing, not because of our merit but because of His grace.

Regardless, Isaac called his favorite son Esau and asked him to prepare a delicious meal, and then Isaac would give him the blessing. But when Jacob came in dressed up like Esau to receive the blessing, Isaac unknowingly gave it to him. Isaac blessed

Jacob and asked God to give him provision and abundant crops (Genesis 27:28). Isaac beseeched the Lord to cause many people, including Esau, to serve Jacob. And Isaac extended God's precious Abrahamic covenant to his younger son Jacob, asking God to bless those who blessed him, and curse those who cursed him (27:29).

When Isaac asked God to bless Jacob, the blessing didn't ultimately come from Isaac but from the Lord. Jacob didn't receive the blessing because he was perfect or because his father was perfect, but because Jacob was God's sovereign choice (Romans 9:10–16).

Isaac's final words of blessing to Jacob show us that God's will supersedes ours. And not only that, but His grace surpasses our sin. Even in the face of Isaac's favoritism and of Rebekah's and Jacob's scheming, God still blessed Jacob—because that was His will.

Time after time, throughout the history of God's people, He repeated His promise to bless Abraham, Isaac, Jacob and their descendants, in spite of their disobedience and repeated efforts to thwart His will.

The truth is that none of us deserve God's blessing. At times, even Christians defy God's plan. But God still gives us good things because He is good. Isaac's blessing reminds us that not only does God bless us despite our rebellion, our sovereign Lord often uses our disobedience to achieve His will.

Who are we to question God? Often the Lord decides to bless those we don't deem worthy of His blessing. But we should remember Isaac's last words of blessing, which accomplished God's will even though all the parties involved disobeyed Him. We, too, have received God's blessing and grace even though we don't always obey Him. But we often demand others to live in perfection in order to receive our love. And if someone violates our trust or hurts our feelings, we give that person the cold shoulder because we think he or she deserves it. Instead, Christians should extend forgiveness and trust that God will even use their cruel actions to achieve His plan (Matthew 6:12–15; Romans 9:20–24).

As Christians, God has chosen to give us His blessing, not because of our merit but because of His grace. In response to God's blessing, believers should live obedient, grace-filled lives that reflect the gift they have received through Christ. "Therefore, since we receive a kingdom which cannot be shaken, let us show gratitude, by which we may offer to God an acceptable service with reverence and awe" (Hebrews 12:28).

Christians live under God's special favor and His unconditional grace. God has included us with the covenant and blessing He gave to Abraham thousands of years ago. God has blessed all people through the salvation that has come from Abraham's seed—Jesus Christ (Galatians 3:16–18). The Lord's gift to us of every spiritual blessing rests on us because of what Christ has done, not because we deserve it. Remember that God "has saved us and called us with a holy calling, not according to our works, but according to His own purpose and grace which was granted us in Christ Jesus from all eternity" (2 Timothy 1:9). God blesses whom He chooses to bless, in spite of their disobedience, because that's His will. Period.

— *Malia Rodriguez*

JACOB'S CONFIDENCE

Born just after his twin brother, Esau, Jacob first opened his eyes to life in a land of promise. Ensured to Jacob's grandfather, Abraham, and guaranteed again to Jacob's father, Isaac, the Promised Land served as a constant, visible reminder of God's provision and faithfulness. Jacob's every step on the firm ground beneath his feet solidified in his mind the reliability of God and His Word.

The twins aged. Jacob bought his older brother's birthright for a pot of stew, leading Esau to despise Jacob's privileged position in the family (Genesis 25:29–34). Esau then fell into sin by taking foreign wives (26:34–35). Jacob's mother, Rebekah, grieved Esau's decisions and therefore plotted with the younger twin to get Jacob the traditional "older brother" blessing from the boys' father, Isaac (Genesis 27:6–10). Esau's grudge against Jacob for his deception made it difficult for Jacob to remain at home. Furthermore, Rebekah wanted to see Jacob married within their tribe, rather than to a foreigner. So Isaac instructed Jacob to leave home in search of a wife.

When Jacob departed, he left with the confidence that God would return him to his homeland. Jacob received assurances—first from his father, Isaac, and then from God Himself (28:1–4, 14–15) — that he and his descendants would dwell in the Promised Land. In Bethel, Jacob responded with his own declaration of confidence in God, setting up a stone pillar — a traditional practice in that time to express one's trust in God. In his journey to find a wife, young Jacob traveled northeast from Beersheba in southern Canaan to his uncle's home in Haran, Paddan-Aram, in what is now southeastern Turkey.

Just as God had assured him, Jacob returned to the Promised Land with numerous household members in tow, and God changed Jacob's name to Israel. The Lord spoke to Jacob once again in Bethel and affirmed that the Abrahamic promise of land and descendants would indeed be fulfilled through Jacob (35:9–12). The land was central to Jacob's sense of his own identity. Not only was the Promised Land the location of his birth, but the land was a tangible guarantee of his family's future. That Jacob lived in the land at all — among Canaanites who had strongholds and armies of their own — would have encouraged him that God would follow through on His promises for numerous descendants in succeeding generations as well as His promise of a life of blessing for Jacob.

Jacob's exit from and return to the land serve as an invaluable context for the end of the patriarch's life. In the midst of a devastating famine, Jacob and his eleven sons moved to Egypt where a twelfth son, Joseph, was in charge of food distribution. With Joseph's political connections, Jacob's extended family received an excellent plot of land to set up house. While this was all a certain blessing in a time when many people starved due to famine, Jacob neared death without the prospect that he or his children would return to live in the Promised Land in the near future.

Jacob's impending death prompted him to speak to his sons. While he would go on to make predictions about their futures, he opened his address with a short, general word of blessing to his family. In essence, Jacob gave his exiled children the same word of confidence he had received as a young man from his father, Isaac, and from God Himself: "God will be with you, and bring you back to the land of your fathers" (Genesis 48:21). While Jacob addressed this final statement to Joseph and Joseph's household — the "you" is plural in Hebrew — Joseph would have never advocated a return to the Promised Land without his extended family. A promise to the generous and conscientious Joseph was a promise to the entire family.

Jacob's last words raise at least three interesting points that

believers today would be wise to reflect upon. First, Jacob's promise to his children rested on God's revealed words to him. Jacob could only make such a promise because he lived so much of his life clinging to God's promise to him. God has made promises to believers today as well. We should order our lives around His promises to us, rather than use other filters — such as feelings or circumstances — to point the way forward.

Jacob died after reminding his family of God's care and trustworthiness — a powerful testimony to anyone who receives it.

Second, Jacob's promise to his children mirrored the promise that his father Isaac had passed on to him so many years before. In other words, Jacob lived his life in deference to his forefathers. We live in a world that casts tradition aside and values individuality. A healthy dose of Jacob-inspired faithfulness to our Christian heritage is much needed.

Third, Jacob died after reminding his family of God's care and trustworthiness — a powerful testimony to anyone who receives it. Even as Jacob fought off the greatest enemy of all humanity — death — first and foremost on his mind was the way that God would care for Jacob's family. The dying man's confidence in God's care and concern for His people remains a powerful testimony of remaining faithful and others-focused to the end.

Our God keeps His promises. He did so with Jacob. He does so with us. May we appreciate the faithfulness of God to keep His Word and to care for His people — just as He has done throughout the generations.

— *John Adair*

JOSEPH'S HOPE

"God will surely take care of you, and you shall carry my bones up from here."

— Genesis 50:25

God wove a beautiful thread through the mottled tapestry of Joseph's life — the thread of hope. From God's plan to use Joseph to provide for his family to the Lord's apparent absence when Joseph's brothers sold him into slavery . . . from Joseph's imprisonment to his elevation to royalty, Joseph put his hope in God's faithfulness. Throughout the twists and turns of Providence, Joseph held on to the Lord's promise to Abraham, Isaac, and Jacob to give His people the land of Canaan (Genesis 12:1–3;15:18; 35:9–12). Joseph knew that God would care for, help, and protect His people as He fulfilled this promise. And with his dying words, Joseph fervently reminded his family members — and believers today — to hope in God's faithful promises, even when tempted by circumstances to doubt.

When Joseph was a teenager, the Lord gave him two prophetic dreams, both of which foretold his rule over his brothers and parents (Genesis 37:5–11). Joseph's dreams incited jealousy and hatred in his brothers' hearts, so they sold him into Egyptian slavery. But God sent Joseph to the house of Pharaoh's chief bodyguard, Potiphar (37:36) — one step closer to his destiny as his family's savior. God's grace was so evident in Joseph's life that Potiphar elevated him to master of Potiphar's house.

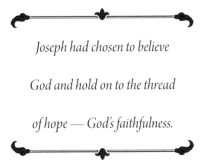

Joseph had chosen to believe God and hold on to the thread of hope — God's faithfulness.

Joseph thrived in Egypt . . . until Potiphar's wife falsely accused Joseph of sexual assault (39:19–20). Where was God when Joseph was cast into jail, for a number of years, for a crime he didn't commit? Right there with him, as He had always been. As the prison doors slammed shut,

Joseph had nothing to cling to but his hope in God's promise.

At long last, Joseph was given a chance to interpret Pharaoh's dream and was subsequently promoted to second-in-command over all Egypt. Joseph recognized that through the loops and knots in the fabric of his life, God had kept His promise to elevate him above his brothers and parents. And if God could keep His promise to Joseph, surely God would keep His promise to His people.

Fast-forward to the great famine that God had revealed previously through the interpretation of Pharaoh's dream. Joseph, Pharaoh's right-hand man and the one in charge of managing the food reserves in Egypt, was in a position to provide for his family, who otherwise might have starved. And later, as Joseph looked back at his life, he knew that God had providentially directed his steps so that through him God could save a remnant of His people and one day settle them in the land He had promised to Abraham (50:20–21).

Finally, after 110 years of walking with the Lord, Joseph had accumulated a wealth of wisdom. So with his final words, Joseph reminded his family to hope in the Lord's faithfulness, for surely the Lord would care for them, as He always had, until the promise He had made to Abraham, Isaac, and Jacob came to fruition (Genesis 50:24). Joseph had so much confidence in God's promise to give His people the Promised Land that Joseph made his brothers swear an oath to take his bones to Canaan!

In Joseph's last words, we discover the secret to his hope-filled, faithful life. Joseph's father had taught him about the unconditional covenant God had made with Abraham, to give him and his descendants the land of Canaan. And when Jacob was about to die, the patriarch extended God's promise to Joseph and his sons (48:15–16). Joseph had chosen to believe God and hold on to the thread of hope — God's faithfulness. Through the ups and downs of his life, Joseph had focused on God's continual presence and His eternal promise. And with his dying breath, Joseph charged his family to do the same (50:24–25).

How has the Lord cared for you by displaying His faithfulness in your life? God often provides the clearest evidence of His help and the firmest anchor of hope in the midst of trials. So the next time the winds and waves slam against your life, pick up your Bible and find hope in God's promises. God has promised Christians a heavenly homeland and resurrection from the grave. The Lord has vowed to breathe eternal life into Joseph's bones and our bones (Ezekiel 37:11–14; John 11:25). But until then, He has promised to be with us, to never forsake us (Deuteronomy 31:6; Matthew 28:19–20), and through the Holy Spirit, to equip us with the power that raised Christ from the dead (Romans 8:11).

We can't put our ultimate hope in people, material things, or achievements. They will all fail us. Enduring hope can only be found in God's promises. When trials or sickness come, when we lose our jobs, and when people reject us, God's faithfulness must be our anchor.

The Lord doesn't promise to remove trials from our lives, but He promises to be with us and to care for us in the midst of them. And after we have experienced His care through His Spirit, His Word, and His people, let's extend His hope to others who desperately need it. Just as the Lord used Joseph to save His people and preserve the promised remnant, God will use us to help others hope in His faithful promises.

— *Malia Rodriguez*

MOSES'S ANTICIPATION

Moses lived his life in anticipation. In his early days, he looked forward to the deliverance of God's people from Egypt. In his later days, Moses's attention turned to taking the nation of Israel back to the Promised Land. Throughout it all, Moses worked to focus the people's eyes on the path leading toward the fulfillment of God's promise.

The Bible introduces Moses as a helpless infant in danger of death due to the command of an overzealous and bloodthirsty Pharaoh. Moses's mother desired the boy's safety, so she laid him in a basket in the Nile River. When Pharaoh's daughter discovered the child, she took pity on him, ensured the child's care, and eventually brought the boy into her home as her son (Exodus 2:10). As young Moses grew up in the house of a foreign and godless king, he remained an outsider, separated from his people. At this point in its history, the nation of Israel was like a boomerang at its furthest point from its thrower and on the verge of returning to its starting point, which for Israel was the land of promise.

Part of Moses's growth into maturity involved his grasping God's vision for the Hebrew people. During those early years that Moses lived in Pharaoh's house, the Lord cultivated in Moses a heart for his own people. However, Moses's desire to see his people free from Egyptian abuse and enslavement led him to perpetrate a rash act of abuse himself—Moses killed an Egyptian who had been beating a Hebrew (Exodus 2:11–12). But the rescue of God's people from Egypt would not come as a result of military tactics or guerrilla violence. God desired to reveal His power and His care for His people in unmistakable fashion.

Pharaoh sought Moses's life for the murder of the Egyptian, leading Moses to seek refuge beyond the Sinai desert in Midian — the desert beyond the desert. Many years in this lonely region could not make Moses forget his people. Neither could he forget the promise of an abundant and blessed land that God had given to the Hebrews. Moses even named his son Gershom, meaning "a foreigner there," as a reminder that he had been sojourning in a foreign land (2:22).

After forty years of shepherding flocks in Midian, Moses found himself near the mountain where God would one day reveal His Ten Commandments (3:1; Acts 7:30). On this day, though, God gave only one command: He wanted Moses to return to Egypt and tell Pharaoh, in the name of God, to release God's people from captivity. Moses had clung to the promise of God his whole life. But only now, at eighty years old and in the middle of nowhere, decades after Moses had been anywhere near God's people, did the Lord confirm that promise in a way that Moses could not mistake. God, too, had a desire to see His people released from captivity.

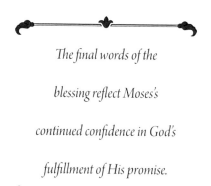

The final words of the blessing reflect Moses's continued confidence in God's fulfillment of His promise.

Of course, we are familiar with those famous highlights from the life of Moses—his courageous appearances before Pharaoh, his leading God's people out of Egypt and through the Red Sea, and his receiving the Ten Commandments on Mount Sinai. However, it was in a quieter moment in the desert, as the people wandered in punishment for their disobedience, that the Lord told Moses he would not actually enter the Promised Land. A moment of weakness, revealing Moses's lack of trust to honor God in a specific way, would keep Moses from personally stepping into the land (Numbers 20:12). However, Moses's vision for the land would continue to burn brightly and serve as a guide for the people

as he led them right up to their promised inheritance.

Just before the people entered the land, leaving Moses behind, the now 120-year-old leader stood up to remind the people of God's Law. His sermon, which comprises the book of Deuteronomy, ends with Moses's famous last words: a song (Deuteronomy 32:1–43) and a blessing (33:1–29). The final words of the blessing reflect Moses's continued confidence in God's fulfillment of His promise:

> "Blessed are you,
>   O Israel;
> Who is like you, a
>   people saved by the
>   Lord?
> Who is the shield of
>   your help
> And the sword of your
>   majesty!
> So your enemies will
>   cringe before you,
> And you will tread
>   upon their high
>   places." (33:29)

These words prompted their hearers to be grateful for the land which the Lord would soon provide, land that would have been in sight by this time. The words reminded the people that God would indeed accompany them into the land and lay waste the enemies before them.

Moses's anticipation of the fulfillment of God's promise never wavered. Moses clung to that vision both before God revealed Himself at the burning bush and afterward. And in this, the old leader of Israel serves as a potent example to us. Christians today are the recipients of a special promise, one that should color with anticipation everything we see in the world. We believe that Jesus will return and make all things new. We believe in a world to come with no more pain or sorrow or death. That we believe in this world to come should guide our steps in the world today. Will we live in light of God's good promise to His people by bringing life and joy and healing to the people in our lives?

— *John Adair*

JOSHUA'S CHOICE

"Choose for yourselves

today whom you will serve:

whether the gods which

your fathers served which

were beyond the River, or

the gods of the Amorites

in whose land you are

living; but as for me

and my house, we will

serve the LORD."

—Joshua 24:15

F ew choices last a lifetime. Most require daily, deliberate reminders. Joshua knew this well.

Immediately after Joshua and the young nation of Israel entered the Promised Land, they made a beeline to a particular valley between two mountains. God commanded half the people to stand before one mountain and the other half to position itself before the other. Each group was to shout either the blessings or the curses that Israel would experience as a result of their response to God's Law (Deuteronomy 11:29).

As they shouted, their voices echoed in the city of Shechem, which lay in the valley between these hills. Before God's people would conquer and settle the land, they affirmed their obedience to God in the very place where God had promised the land to Abraham (Genesis 12:7). The significance of the place served to strengthen their commitment.

Years later, after Joshua and the twelve tribes had control of the Holy Land, Joshua assembled the nation at Shechem — one more time — just before his death.

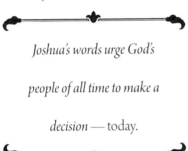

Joshua's words urge God's people of all time to make a decision — today.

There, the elderly leader of God's people reminded them that Abraham first came to the land after leaving a life of idolatry (Joshua 24:2). Joshua rehearsed the history of the young nation, recounting God's tremendous faithfulness and power that had delivered the people. Shechem's significant history and the weight of the Lord's mercy worked in tandem to drive home Joshua's application point: "Now, therefore, fear the Lord and serve Him

in sincerity and truth; and put away the gods which your fathers served beyond the River and in Egypt, and serve the Lord" (24:14).

Twice Joshua gave the command: "serve the Lord" — the principal application of the whole chapter. Serving the Lord "in sincerity and truth" means serving Him completely, consistently, and authentically.

Interestingly, Jesus would say a similar thing in this same location many centuries later. Jesus's name in Hebrew is *Yeshua* — or Joshua. Just around the corner from where His namesake spoke of serving the Lord "in sincerity and truth," Jesus would tell a woman at Jacob's well that the worshipers God seeks are those who worship Him in "spirit and in truth" (John 4:23). Jesus's words would echo Joshua's, referring to complete, consistent, and authentic obedience.

Next in Joshua's final speech to the Israelites came the most famous verse in the book that bears his name:

"If it is disagreeable in your sight to serve the LORD, choose for your-selves today whom you will serve: whether the gods which your fathers served which were beyond the River, or the gods of the Amori-tes in whose land you are living; but as for me and my house, we will serve the LORD."
(Joshua 24:15)

Regrettably, most modern-day wall plaques that quote this verse replace half of it with an ellipsis. Many Christian gift shops assume that the parts about the "gods which your fathers served . . . or the gods of the Amorites in whose land you are living" have no bearing on twenty-first-century believers. How unfortunate!

By principle, Joshua's words urge God's people of all time to make a decision — *today*. We can choose to live the way our parents and grandparents did — following their poor pri-orities and choices. We can also choose to chase the idols of the people in the culture in which we live today. But the best choice? Joshua demonstrated it by exam-ple: "As for me and my house, we will serve the LORD."

Even for those who grew up in Christian homes, the decision still remains a personal one. Every individual needs to come to the place where Jesus is his or her God, not just the God of his or her parents. What's more, although the decision to believe in Jesus occurs one time, the decision to obey Him occurs *today* — and every day. Although some choices last a lifetime, most require daily, deliberate reminders.

Joshua used both history and geography to reignite a dedication to the Lord. We can do the same. What physical reminders can we keep in our lives to act as mem-ory triggers of God's faithfulness to us — a place we pass, a plaque on the wall, a communion cup, a photo album? Simple reminders can prompt us to renew our per-sonal decision to serve the Lord each day. We need these daily reminders in order to renew our minds — to draw us close to God and away from the carnal tugs of our culture.

There's no magic bullet to increase faithfulness. No sanctification pill to swallow. No sermon or study Bible to offer us the "secret" to forever faithfulness. Rather, our dedication to serve the Lord "in sincerity and truth" must occur today — and every day.

Joshua's final message should be words we carry to the end of our own days: "As for me and my house, we will serve the LORD."

— *Wayne Stiles*

SAMSON'S SACRIFICE

"O Lord God, please remember me and please strengthen me just this time, O God, that I may at once be avenged of the Philistines for my two eyes. . . . Let me die with the Philistines!"

— Judges 16:28, 30

The city of Zorah sat upon the crest of a hill on the north side of the Sorek Valley in Israel. From this lofty perch, Zorah's residents sat in a position of stability and security with full command of the valley below. Into this city, a once-barren woman birthed a child who became known for his impressive physical prowess. Not only did this young man, named Samson, possess supernatural strength by the empowering Holy Spirit, but Samson was also blessed with loving parents and a clear purpose in life. The Lord directed Samson's parents to raise the boy as a Nazirite, a person separated unto the service of God (Numbers 6:1–21; Judges 13:4–5).

From the heights of his life in Zorah, Samson descended into the Sorek Valley, which was occupied by Israel's enemy: the

Philistines. Down in the valley, Samson began a life of taking instead of giving. Rather than serve others, Samson looked to serve himself. When desire for a Philistine woman filled Samson's heart, he determined to take her in marriage without consideration of God's prohibitions against marrying foreign women (Deuteronomy 7:3–4). When Samson's father and mother suggested their son find a bride from among their own people, Samson bluntly rejected their suggestion for no other reason than "she looks good to me" (Judges 14:3). And when Samson's stomach growled with hunger, he broke one of his Nazirite vows by reaching into the carcass of a lion to eat some honey (14:9). In each case, Samson was a taker, eschewing wisdom and acting on impulse. Samson's impulsive actions continued, and God used the actions of this easily angered and vengeful man to assault the Philistines (14:19; 15:7–8, 14–15).

After his time in the Sorek Valley, Samson descended again, walking downhill to the coastal city of Gaza. When the Philistines organized against him, Samson ripped away the doors of the city gates and carried them into the mountains. This act exposed the city to invaders and made it clear that Samson was operating with a measure of strength unknown to and beyond any of them. When Samson went back to the Sorek Valley, the Gazites pursued him there and plotted his demise through his newest attraction—Delilah (16:4–5). When Samson gave away the secret of his strength after much pestering from his female companion, the Philistines seized him, gouged out his eyes, and made him a grinder of grain in the prison (16:21).

Blind and weak in a Gazite prison, Samson finally reached his lowest point. Throughout Samson's life, God had used Samson's impulsive behavior and taste for foreign women to punish the godless Philistines. With each new desire he fulfilled, with each new obstacle he overcame, Samson had paid no attention to his God. The man who lived the bulk of his life in obedience to his Nazirite vow (long hair, avoiding wine, avoiding corpses) never matched that outward image of holiness with the substance of an inward commitment to the Lord.

But now, surrounded by walls and darkness, and completely powerless to do anything about it, Samson got his chance at redemption. God gave Samson one opportunity to elevate his life's legacy—ending the lives of Philistines by bringing down their own temple on top of them. As Samson stood in the Philistine temple dedicated to their god, Dagon, he grasped the pillars on either side of him, addressing the true God with his final words: "O Lord God, please remember me and please strengthen me just this time, O God, that I may at once be avenged of the Philistines for my two eyes. . . . Let me die with the Philistines!" (Judges 16:28, 30).

After a lifetime of showing off an image rather than the true substance of following God, Samson received this final opportunity from the Lord. And in that final moment, Samson called upon the Lord for help to bring down the temple, even though it meant

Samson would sacrifice his own life in the process.

Samson spent his entire life as a taker. But he finished his life by giving himself entirely to the service of God and His people. Samson's final words and deeds show us that it is never too late to turn to the Lord. Though he was used of God to battle the Philistines, an observer would be hard-pressed to argue that Samson lived his life well, in accordance with the ways of God. However, Samson most certainly ended well, taking his only opportunity to do something for God rather than for himself.

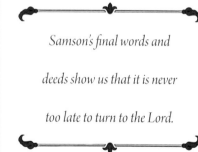

Samson's final words and deeds show us that it is never too late to turn to the Lord.

As a blind prisoner, Samson's options for serving God were few. We may find ourselves in situations where our past choices in life have limited us. Previous sins in our lives also may limit our ability to serve God in every possible capacity today. Samson's story teaches us to take hold of opportunities to serve God in the ways that have been made available to us. Those opportunities may not be ideal. They may even cause us some measure of pain. But God invites us to follow the example of Samson's sacrifice by embracing the next chance we will have to serve the Lord.

— John Adair

AGAG'S NAIVETÉ

"Surely the worst is over, and I have been spared!"

—1 Samuel 15:32 NLT

Blind selfishness leads people into all manner of wickedness. We see it time and again in Scripture. The Amalekites, a people descended from Esau, had a golden opportunity to serve God's people. After the Israelites escaped Egypt, they trekked through the Sinai desert and drew near to the land of the Amalekites. Historically, as descendants of Esau, the Amalekites would have likely had some animosity built up toward Jacob's Israelites, going back to the rivalries of Jacob and Esau in the era of the patriarchs.

Now, the Israelites were moving *en masse* through a desolate area. The opportunity for the Amalekites to show hospitality to strangers was unmistakable. The Amalekites eschewed peace and instead chose aggression—they attacked the traveling Israelites

(Exodus 17:8–16). Moses and Joshua helped to deliver the people from the surprise attack, but the damage was done, at least as far as the Amalekites were concerned. Due to the mistreatment of God's people, the Lord vowed to destroy the people of Amalek (17:14).

About four hundred years after that fateful battle, King Saul reigned over Israel as the nation's first (human) king. While Saul had shown a propensity for foolishness, he had done nothing up to this point to endanger his kingship. In many ways, he served as a capable king to his people, defending them from enemies who attacked Israel on all sides (1 Samuel 14:47). One of those enemies was the Amalekites, who attacked the southern edges of Saul's kingdom, though Saul valiantly defeated them (14:48).

In the midst of making these defenses, Saul received a visit from the aged prophet Samuel. Saul jumped into action upon hearing God's command, via Samuel, to destroy all the Amalekites, including their livestock. God was going to use Saul and the Israelite army to extinguish the Amalekites and fulfill His promise made hundreds of years prior. However, Saul blatantly disobeyed, leaving alive the Amalekite king, Agag, along with a number of livestock that Saul planned to use to make offerings to the Lord (15:9).

. . . we need to cast off the

blissful naiveté of Agag for

the sharp vision of the wise

and discerning.

Samuel arrived on the scene with the righteous anger of the Lord burning in his heart. After the prophet rebuked Saul in the strongest terms for disobeying the Lord, "Samuel said, 'Bring me Agag, the King of the Amalekites'" (15:32). What should have been a moment of pause for the Amalekite king, given the testy rebuke Samuel had just handed out to Saul, was actually nothing of the sort. Agag approached God's prophet with the same arrogance and naiveté that his people had when they attacked Israel in the Sinai desert all those years before. The Bible tells us that "Agag came to him cheerfully. And Agag said, 'Surely the bitterness of death is past'" (1 Samuel 15:32). Agag's naiveté manifested itself as misplaced hope. The Amalekite king's hope was based on untruths about his people's place before God, as well as Agag's inability to see the clear implications of his actions. He simply could not comprehend judgment coming at the hands of the old man before him, especially after his life had been spared by the king! Samuel, however, wasted little time; he grabbed a sword, and "hewed Agag to pieces" (15:33). The judgment of God was complete.

King Agag of Amalek would have fit in well with many of us in the modern-day world—we, like Agag, are adept at telling ourselves stories to rationalize away the negative effects of our choices. And yet, King Agag stands—or better, lays — as a chilling reminder of the impact of our decisions on those closest to us. The judgment on Agag, his people, and his livestock resulted in part from the Amalekite king's continuing actions as an enemy to God's people. But God's judgment was ultimately rooted in the choices made by Agag's ancestors. The choices of those men and women, hundreds of years prior, cemented an antagonistic attitude toward God and His people that never relented during Israel's time in the land.

The effects of generational sin are hard for us to swallow, for they presume that we don't all start life with the same opportunities for success. Each of our families comes tailor-made with its own struggles and hindrances. Some of these troubles are circumstantial, but others come as a direct result of sin — our own sins and the sins of those who have come before us. When we, like Agag, refuse to take a clear-eyed view of our situation, we leave ourselves open to increasing difficulty. For Agag, that meant instant death. For us, it could mean a rift in a special relationship, a court case for a close family member, or an injury or illness that could have been prevented.

Upon sending them out into the world, Jesus told His disciples to "be shrewd as serpents and innocent as doves" (Matthew 10:16). Knowing that we exist in a fallen world where everyone — including ourselves — has been tainted by sin, we need to cast off the blissful naiveté of Agag for the sharp vision of the wise and discerning. When we admit our own failures and selfishness, when we take responsibility for those times when we've taken advantage of others, we take the first step toward living lives that will truly reflect the light of the gospel's good news of salvation and solace.

— *John Adair*

GOLIATH'S FALL

Pride truly does come before a fall— and Goliath fell with a loud, proud thud. Standing more than nine feet tall, Goliath towered over his fellow soldiers. Goliath learned from his earliest days that his size and strength could be used to his advantage. The Philistine army probably recruited Goliath and trained him as their prize fighter. They used his size and strength to their advantage when they faced Saul and the army of Israelites near Socoh (1 Samuel 17:1). Goliath's large frame easily bore the weight of 125 pounds of armor, and he held a spear that weighed more than fifteen pounds (17:5–7).[1]

The Philistines encamped on one mountain and the Israelites on another with the valley of Elah between them (17:2–3). When Goliath, the champion of the Philistines, walked down the mountain and stood in the valley, King Saul shuddered. And when the man from Gath called out, demanding a duel with their strongest fighter, not one of the Israelite soldiers accepted the challenge (1 Samuel 17:11). For forty days and nights, Goliath threatened God's people. Goliath didn't fear the Israelites, and he didn't fear their God.

Goliath didn't fear the Lord but instead trusted in his own ability to make things happen.

But finally, one young man stepped up to the challenge. David, a shepherd by trade, grew tired of watching God's people live in fear. So David volunteered to fight Goliath, armed with a slingshot, a few stones, and God's power. But Goliath didn't recognize the spiritual weapon at David's disposal. So with his last words, Goliath mocked David

and God. Goliath called on his "gods" and cursed David. The giant proudly exclaimed: "Come to me, and I will give your flesh to the birds of the sky and the beasts of the field" (17:44). Little did Goliath know, the humble man with God on his side would soon cut off Goliath's head and give his flesh to the birds and beasts.

All it took was one fist-sized rock to fell the prize fighter, Goliath—not just because David had good aim but because David trusted God's promise to fight for His people and defeat their enemies (17:47). David rebuked Goliath, who in pride had set himself up against the one true God. David said: "You come to me with a sword, a spear, and a javelin, but I come to you in the name of the Lord of hosts, the God of the armies of Israel, whom you have taunted" (17:45).

So what can believers learn from the pagan, Goliath, who put his hope in his physical strength instead of in God? Christians must remember that God resists the proud and He opposes those who refuse to submit to Him (1 Peter 5:5). The apostle Peter's words remind Christians not to relate to one another with a prideful spirit by putting our own needs and desires before those of others. But if we do, God will resist or work against us, desiring us to repent. Pride won't cause us to lose our salvation, but it will result in God's loving and sometimes painful discipline. How tragic for believers to live life with God working against them because of their pride!

We can also learn that fearing the Lord leads to wisdom and true strength. But when we fear people or circumstances, we display spiritual weakness. Goliath didn't trust the God of Israel, but neither did King Saul and most of the Israelite army. Goliath's size and strength paralyzed them, and they refused to trust that God could defeat Goliath and the Philistine army. But David's fear of the Lord allowed him to exercise the courage and wisdom he needed to face Goliath. Likewise, we must trust God to give us resolutions to our problems rather than relying merely

on our common sense or popular solutions. God allows us to face obstacles, not to cause us to fear but to develop our humility and dependence on Him.

Finally, Goliath set himself up against God and His people. As an unbeliever, Goliath trusted in his own ability to make things happen. When we make our own plans and set out to achieve them by whatever means possible, we are living as the world lives. As Christ followers, we must submit our plans to the Lord and wait for His clear guidance (Psalm 37:5). Just as Jesus laid His will and His life at the Father's feet, we must do the same (Matthew 26:39). And if the Lord has given us guidance to follow a certain path but we refuse to follow Him, we set ourselves up against God. However, God will achieve His plans with or without us.

What plans have we refused to submit to the Lord? In what ways have we attempted to make our plans work by our own efforts? Has pride infiltrated our relationships with others, causing us to view ourselves as more important? The fear of the Lord leads to wisdom, and humility must precede honor (Proverbs 15:33). But pride, even in the heart of a Christian, will inevitably lead to a fall. Our heavenly Father loves us so much that He will allow us to fall so that we will humble ourselves and yield to His will (3:11–12). As always, God's will is best. But the question is: Do we really trust Him?

— *Malia Rodriguez*

1.   C. P. Weber, "Goliath," in *The Zondervan Pictorial Encyclopedia of the Bible*, vol. 2, *D – G*, gen. ed. Merrill C. Tenney (Grand Rapids: Zondervan, 1975, 1976), 774.

SAUL'S FEARFULNESS

"Draw your sword

and pierce me through

with it, otherwise these

uncircumcised will come

and pierce me through and

make sport of me."

—1 Samuel 31:4

Some people start with all the advantages in the world—a good family, stature in the community, and a striking physical appearance. As the Bible makes clear time and again, however, where we end always trumps where we begin. The life of Israel's first king, Saul—who was chosen by God to allay the people's fear of other nations (1 Samuel 8:19–20)—provides a chilling reminder of this biblical truth.

The Bible introduces Saul through his father, Kish. The broader community in and around Gibeah knew Kish as a man of valor (9:1). Kish carried a sterling military reputation in his town. Strength, toughness, and perseverance marked his character. This man, known primarily for his courage and bravery in the heat of battle, reared the first king of Israel.

Growing up in the home of a hero, Saul would have been known in the area. His handsome looks and exceptional height increased the attention that came with his family connections (1 Samuel 9:2). Saul looked the part of a man of valor, but deep within, he was always a man of fear.

The prophet and judge, Samuel, who led Israel at the time of Saul's rise to the throne, privately anointed Saul to the kingship (9:27–10:1). Sometime later, Samuel publicly announced Saul's new position as king, and in this moment the people received the first hint that their new king would not measure up to his illustrious, valorous father. As Samuel called for Saul, silence answered. No one knew where to find the new king. He had disappeared. Samuel asked the Lord where he could find Saul, and God responded that Saul was "hiding himself by the baggage" (10:22). In this moment of great import for Israel, a moment Saul already knew would play out with him announced as king and ruler over his people, the Benjamite

cowered in the shadows and lost himself in the luggage. That the people had to retrieve him from his hiding place and bring him to the prophet only served to underscore the crippling fear within this young man whom God had chosen as the people's king.

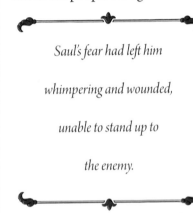

Saul's fear had left him

whimpering and wounded,

unable to stand up to

the enemy.

Over the course of his long reign, Saul often acted in accordance with his fearful nature. On one occasion not long after his anointing, the king gathered his army and prepared to battle tens of thousands of Philistines at Gilgal. However, before the battle, the prophet Samuel planned to make an offering in order to seek the Lord's blessing on the fight. Saul was to wait at Gilgal seven days for Samuel to arrive. In the meantime, Israel's army began to hide themselves, terrified by the sight of the massive Philistine force arrayed before them. When Samuel didn't arrive promptly on the seventh day, the king began to quail. In an effort to keep his army from fleeing the coming fight, Saul himself made the offering. The king took on the role of priest, appointing himself as mediator between God and His people. Samuel arrived soon afterward and rebuked Saul for his foolishness (1 Samuel 13:8–13).

Saul continued to fail his kingdom by entertaining and acting upon his fears. He feared his own people in the aftermath of their battle with the Amalekites (15:24). He feared for his own kingship as David's successes grew (18:28–29). Saul also feared for his own life against the Philistines, which prompted him to seek out a medium (28:5–7). These fears paved a wide road of selfishness and idolatry, a road that led directly to Saul's death. During a battle with the Philistines, with three of his sons already slain on the slopes of Mount Gilboa, the king was wounded and cornered. In this tragic moment, Saul "groaned" his final words to his armor bearer, "Draw your sword and pierce me through with it, otherwise these uncircumcised will come and pierce me through and make sport of me" (31:4).

Saul had once been at the pinnacle of God's nation, born in a respected family and with the greatest power in the universe at his back. However, by choosing a life of fear, he let it all slip away, finally so afraid that he commanded a subordinate to kill him. Saul's fear had left him whimpering and wounded, unable to stand up to the enemy. Though the armor bearer refused to kill the king, Saul killed himself before the Philistines could arrive to do the job. For Saul, cowardice in life led to cowardice in death.

As God's people, we look at Saul's life as a cautionary tale. Apart from God's grace, we all would end up as quivering masses of fear. But as believers, people indwelt by the Holy Spirit, we recognize that "God has not given us a spirit of timidity, but of power and love and discipline" (2 Timothy 1:7). God has not made us a people of fear. He has not created us to cower at threats of violence or shrink at the thought of a changing world. Rather, God has made us a people who can draw upon the power of the Spirit for courage in the face of terrible threats and for determination in light of paralyzing anxieties. May Saul's example remind us of who we're not as well as who we are.

— *John Adair*

DAVID'S VISION

"I am going the way of all the earth. Be strong, therefore, and show yourself a man. Keep the charge of the LORD your God, to walk in His ways … according to what is written in the Law of Moses, that you may succeed in all that you do and wherever you turn."

—1 Kings 2:2–3

Living life with vision requires the ability to see beyond our immediate circumstances and base our actions on something more stable than a feeling or a quickly developing event. As a young man and as king, David effectively applied this principle. The man after God's own heart regularly acted with a longer view in mind, making sacrificial or dangerous decisions because he held firmly to higher principles that were more important than his own freedom or safety. Following God in obedience was primary for David, whatever the consequences for himself.

Prior to taking over the reign of Israel, David made several striking decisions that placed him squarely in the crosshairs of wickedness. When his father sent him to take food to his older brothers who were serving on the front lines of a war with the Philistines, David inserted himself into the battle without thought for his own preservation. The intimidating figure of Goliath stood opposite the young king-to-be, but David stood strong. Defending the honor of the Lord

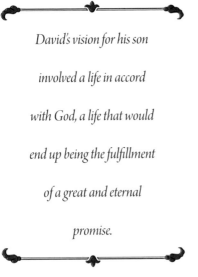

David's vision for his son

involved a life in accord

with God, a life that would

end up being the fulfillment

of a great and eternal

promise.

and His people was more important than huddling in the safety and security of the army. Finding strength in the name of the Lord, David defeated the giant — and the Philistines — with one sling of a stone (1 Samuel 17:45–49).

David also defended the Lord's honor while on the run from Saul. In this case, David accomplished the task, not by killing an enemy but by refusing to kill a former friend, King Saul.

David had an opportunity to kill Saul when Saul unknowingly entered the cave where David and his men were hiding (24:1–7). David resisted taking action against the king, even against the pleas of his men. Concern for the Lord motivated David's choice. In a moment when David could have sped up his ascent to the throne of Israel, the young man avoided a rash action and instead waited on the Lord to act decisively on his behalf.

Some time later, David and Abishai sneaked into Saul's camp under cover of night. Standing right next to Israel's king, David again resisted a friend's encouragement to kill Saul, instead expressing trust in the Lord to deliver them from Saul's pursuit (26:6–11). Here again David eschewed the easy path before him for the more difficult path of trusting God's sovereign hand to work out His plan. David was content to follow God's explicit commands, rather than create opportunities to serve God through commands of dubious, self-serving origin.

In every one of these instances, all taking place before David ever ascended the throne, the young man sought to direct his life according to God's ways and desires rather than his own. While David faltered and sinned at various times during his reign as king, he generally lived a life oriented toward walking in the Lord's ways.

This concern in David's life is revealed in his final words, spoken to his son Solomon:

> "I am going the way of all the earth. Be strong, therefore, and show yourself a man. Keep the charge of the LORD your God, to walk in His ways, to keep His statutes, His commandments, His ordinances, and His testimonies, according to what is written in the Law of Moses, that you may succeed in all that you do and wherever you turn, so that the LORD may carry out His promise which He spoke concerning me, saying, 'If your sons are careful of their way, to walk before Me in truth with all their heart and with all their soul, you shall not lack a man on the throne of Israel.'" (1 Kings 2:2–4)

In this passage, David expressed to his son the importance of keeping the commandments of God. Obedience, David knew, would be key for Solomon as he continued leading Israel in the positive direction taken by David. The king's final concern for his son revolved around a life well-lived. Deeds, not words, would determine where Israel would head under Solomon. When David followed up with instructions for Solomon regarding specific people (2:5–9), it became clear that obedience to God's commands would involve Solomon performing specific actions while seeking specific results. David's vision for his son involved a life in accord with God, a life that would end up being the fulfillment of a great and eternal promise.

While David's final words had particular significance for Solomon, they speak to the lives of people today as well. David equated obedience to the Lord's commands with being "strong" and showing oneself "a man," or a person of courage (1 Kings 2:2). David understood that walking consistently in God's ways leads a person to spiritual maturity. Manhood or womanhood, by God's design, begins by living a life of obedience to God. That was true for Solomon, and it remains true for all of us. Whether or not we find ourselves in positions of leadership, we need to adopt David's vision for ourselves. When we do so, we will find our lives on the path to fulfilling God's promise to us in Christ: eternal life and transformation into mature human beings, pleasing to God.

— John Adair

ELIJAH'S LEGACY

"You have asked a hard thing. Nevertheless, if you see me when I am taken from you, it shall be so for you; but if not, it shall not be so."

—2 Kings 2:10

Elijah could see despair, anxiety, and anticipation in his young protégé's eyes. He had tried to distance himself from Elisha to prepare him for his departure. But Elisha refused to leave Elijah's side. Elisha couldn't bear the thought that he would be left *alone* as God's prophet. Sensing the enormity of the transition, Elijah wanted to leave a legacy for Elisha so his ministry would bear fruit.

Elijah had cared for Elisha like a son. So, before he was swept up in a heavenly whirlwind, Elijah asked what he could do for Elisha. He wanted to equip his successor with the spiritual tools he needed to fill Elijah's prophetic shoes. So whatever Elisha needed—wisdom, insight, anything—Elijah wanted to give that to him. To the end, Elijah concerned himself first and foremost with the continuing work of the Lord.

As Elijah's spiritual son and heir in ministry, Elisha asked for a double portion, not of Elijah's material possessions as was the right of the firstborn son, but of Elijah's spiritual power. So with his last words, Elijah addressed this difficult request. Elijah said: "You have asked a hard thing. Nevertheless, if you see me when I am taken from you, it shall be so for you; but if not, it shall not be so" (2 Kings 2:10).

But what did Elijah mean when he said that Elisha's request would be difficult to grant? And why did Elisha have to watch Elijah as the heavenly chariots took him to heaven? And what does the legacy of Elijah mean for believers today?

Elisha's request for a double portion of Elijah's spirit was really a request for the Holy Spirit to work mightily through Elisha as he had seen the Spirit work through Elijah. Elijah had understood that his spiritual power came from the Lord, not from his own abilities.

As the prophet appointed by God to discipline and convict evil King Ahab, Elijah had trusted the Lord to preserve his life every day (1 Kings 17:1–6). When a famine hit Israel and the Lord told Elijah that a poor, starving widow would provide food and water for him,

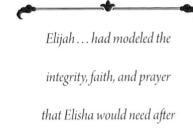

Elijah ... had modeled the

integrity, faith, and prayer

that Elisha would need after

Elijah was gone.

Elijah had trusted that the Lord would miraculously provide for both of them (17:13–14). And when Elijah stood alone on Mount Carmel and faced 450 prophets of Baal, he knew God would come through for him. When Elijah challenged the pagan priests to a sacrifice-burning duel, he trusted that the Lord would display His unmatched power in the sight of all the people (18:36–40).

Elijah had lived his entire life as a prophet who relied on the

Lord's power working through him. So it would not just be hard, but impossible, for Elijah to give Elisha power that belonged to God. But Elijah, who trusted his calling as a prophet and who knew that God had chosen Elisha as his successor (1 Kings 19:19), had faith that God would give Elisha whatever spiritual fortitude he needed to carry out his prophetic calling.

But before Elisha learned whether he would receive the double portion of spiritual power he had asked for, he had to keep his eyes focused on Elijah. Why? Because as Elisha watched the flaming chariots from heaven lift Elijah from the earth in a whirlwind, he would witness God's power at work. Elijah had served as Elisha's spiritual guide and mentor in ministry and had modeled the integrity, faith, and prayer that Elisha would need after Elijah was gone. Elisha had learned from Elijah how to see with spiritual eyes and to remember that the Lord's angels outnumbered Elisha's enemies (2 Kings 6:16–17). And with Elijah's last words, Elisha learned

only God could equip him for the ministry to which God had called him.

So what can Christians today learn from Elijah's last words? We must learn that the power to change lives comes from the Lord, not from us. When the Lord calls us to a difficult task, the Holy Spirit will equip us to achieve it. And like Elijah, we must humble ourselves before the Lord and trust that He will achieve His will according to His own pleasure. So if the time comes for us to step down from a leadership position at work or in ministry, let's pray for our successors and remember that the power to accomplish any task comes from God. When we hold on to our positions after it's time for us to leave, we display our pride and our belief that we alone can fulfill our role. And we may even prevent our successors from growing in their faith as God works through them.

We can also learn from Elijah's last words—and his entire life—that though we face challenges that knock the wind out of us, God responds when we humble ourselves and pray (Matthew 7:7–11). Our heavenly Father has the power either to change our circumstances or to give us the strength to endure them so we can grow to maturity (James 1:2–3).

As Christians, our role is to leave a legacy of faith by modeling integrity, by relying on the Holy Spirit to equip us for ministry, and by inspiring others to trust God. Elijah lived a life of godliness knowing that Elisha was watching him and modeling his life after his. With his famous last words, Elijah released his prophetic ministry to his successor, trusting in God's ability to empower Elisha to accomplish God's will. May we all live with the humility, integrity, and faith of Elijah, and may we pass on that legacy to others.

— *Malia Rodriguez*

ATHALIAH'S AUTHORITY

Then Athaliah tore her

clothes and said,

"Treason! Treason!"

—2 *Chronicles 23:13*

Paranoia goes hand-in-hand with absolute power. And to a heartless dictator, treason is a capital offense. From Stalin to Hitler, Pol Pot to Kim Jong-Il, most dictators will do anything to keep their power—*anything*. They will surround themselves with hordes of armed bodyguards, imprison their opponents, and exile their rivals. Dictators call the shots. They refuse to bow to anyone—especially God. They will even murder family members who are seen as a threat to their power. And that's exactly what Athaliah, queen of Judah, did.

Athaliah, granddaughter of King Omri of Israel and daughter of King Ahab of Israel, married Jehoram (2 Kings 8:16–18), the eldest son of King Jehoshaphat of Judah. The union of Athaliah and Jehoram was merely political. Queen Athaliah influenced Jehoram to worship the gods of King Ahab and to rebel against the God of Jehoshaphat. In his first act as king, Jehoram killed all of his brothers to secure his power (2 Chronicles 21:4), a move likely encouraged by Athaliah. Athaliah's sons would later pillage articles from God's temple and use them to worship Baal (24:7).

The fear of the Lord leads

to wisdom, to submission to

God's sovereignty, and

to humility.

When Ahaziah succeeded his father, Jehoram, as king of Judah, his mother Athaliah served as his counselor (22:3). But deep inside, she wanted full power. Athaliah, an expert in idol worship and self-seeking behavior, influenced King Ahaziah to live an evil, godless life. Less than one year later, God executed judgment on King Ahaziah and

directed Jehu to kill him — which Jehu did (22:8–9).

But Athaliah didn't mourn Ahaziah's death. With her son out of the way, Athaliah was one step away from becoming the sovereign. She devised a fail-safe plan to ensure no other potential successors would arise and strip her of power—she murdered them all. With no apparent competition for control, Queen Athaliah ruled over Judah for six years — an exploit performed by no other female in the history of Judah. But God did not approve of her fanatic ambition . . . and unbeknownst to Athaliah, Jehoiada the priest and his wife, Jehoshabeath, had kept hidden in the temple one of Ahaziah's sons, Joash.

Jehoiada organized a royal ceremony and an army of protectors, and he established Joash, the Lord's anointed, on the throne. When Queen Athaliah heard the commotion and the people yelling, "Long live King Joash," she ran to the temple (23:11–12). If she had had a loyal army with her, Athaliah surely would have tried to murder young King Joash and any others who threatened her power. But Jehoiada the priest charged the military leaders to kill Athaliah and any others who followed her. In her very short swan song, Athaliah was heard crying out, "Treason! Treason!" (2 Chronicles 23:13).

Though Queen Athaliah viewed Jehoiada as the enemy and all the Levites as traitors, she had committed the ultimate treason. By murdering Ahaziah's sons, taking power into her own hands, and rejecting the Lord's new king, she had stationed herself against the true, heavenly King. And she paid for her treachery with her life. Athaliah spoke her final words, "Treason! Treason!" against Jehoiada, Joash, and all those who wanted her out of power. But, truly, Athaliah's last words described her own relationship with God.

Those who, like Athaliah, claw their way to the top, crushing everyone beneath them, clearly have not bowed to the Sovereign Lord. The fear of the Lord stands in total opposition to the fear of losing personal power. Instead, the fear of the Lord leads to wisdom, to submission to God's sovereignty, and to humility. As Christians who acknowledge God's providence and His power to accomplish His will, we bow to Him and submit our wills to His. We declare, as did King Nebuchadnezzar, another despot consumed with his own supremacy, whom God humbled:

> "For His dominion
>   is an everlasting
>   dominion,
> And His kingdom
>   endures from genera-
>   tion to generation.
> All the inhabitants
>   of the earth are
>   accounted as nothing,
> But He does according
>   to His will in the host
>   of heaven
> And among the inhabit-
>   ants of earth;
> And no one can ward
>   off His hand
> Or say to Him, 'What
>   have You done?'"
>   (Daniel 4:34–35)

The majority of us may not hold leadership positions as lofty as Athaliah's, but some Christians do exercise authority over others, as elected officials, ministry leaders, administrators, and business executives. Only when we acknowledge God as sovereign over all things will we lead others with the wisdom and humility that result from godly fear. A Christlike leader would never, in the name of *ambition*, resort to manipulation or step on others to achieve or keep control. If the Lord allows us to exercise a measure of power over others, let's wield it with grace and justice, remembering that God will hold us accountable. And, unlike Athaliah, let's yield our authority when the Lord chooses to elevate someone else above us.

Whether or not we "rule" over others in an official capacity, all Christ-followers must submit heart, mind, and will to the Lord and remember that God has absolute power over every aspect of our lives. Each believer must evaluate his or her heart and ask: *Have I refused to yield any area of my life to God's sovereign control? Or have I, deep in my soul, accused the Lord of treason?* If the answer is yes, we can bow to Him and acknowledge His kingship over everything — over our hopes, fears, dreams, and relationships. It's much less painful to humble ourselves before God than to wait until He humbles us.

— *Malia Rodriguez*

SOLOMON'S WISDOM

The conclusion, when all has been heard, is: fear God and keep His commandments, because this applies to every person. For God will bring every act to judgment, everything which is hidden, whether it is good or evil.

—Ecclesiastes 12:13–14

Ask most students of Scripture about King Solomon, and something about wisdom invariably receives mention. And rightly so—Solomon's wisdom stands as a significant element of his life. Because many consider wisdom to be Solomon's defining characteristic, the impact of his unfaithfulness to God rarely merits consideration. A closer look at Solomon's life finds that his most significant lesson in wisdom came near the end of his life.

When he became king of Israel, Solomon first sought wisdom from God in an encounter the young man had in a dream (1 Kings 3:5–9). Specifically, the new king desired the wisdom to govern God's people—to discern good from evil as he led them. God, in His grace, granted Solomon's request, endowing Solomon with "a wise and discerning heart" (1 Kings 3:12). Solomon illustrated his gift repeatedly. He judged well the disputes between Israelites (3:25), built a temple for the Lord, and brokered peace with the surrounding nations. However, while Solomon possessed wisdom as a leader of God's people, he turned the attentive eye of wisdom away from his own house.

Before Solomon's wisdom dream, he had taken Pharaoh's daughter as a bride. Uniting himself with a woman who did not follow the true God revealed a fundamental weakness in Solomon. In fact, this weakness for women of all kinds led the young king to accumulate them like a jeweler hordes diamonds. Later in his life, Solomon found himself married to or connected with one thousand women, many of them foreign and therefore outside God's desire for His people (11:1–3). These women turned Solomon's heart from the Lord, and he worshiped the gods of other nations.

God has never tolerated idolatry among His people. He prohibited it in the Ten Commandments (Exodus 20:3), and He brought about judgment for it throughout the early centuries of Israel's history. In line with His character, the Lord took swift action with Solomon as well—the king of Israel would lose most of his kingdom, though God only allowed it to happen once Solomon died, for the sake of his father David (1 Kings 11:11–13). What had been the greatest kingdom in the world, drawing the attention of foreign dignitaries while standing as a beacon for the true God, had been rotting from the inside out as a result of Solomon's poor choices.

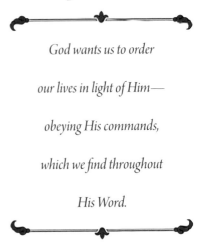

God wants us to order

our lives in light of Him—

obeying His commands,

which we find throughout

His Word.

Experience teaches hard lessons. For all the wisdom God granted him upon ascending to the throne of Israel, Solomon still had to learn the hard way one of the most fundamental human truths. This piece of true and abiding wisdom did not settle in Solomon's heart until his last days on earth.

An aging ruler over a crumbling kingdom, King Solomon sat down to pen Ecclesiastes. The old king reflected bitterly on the pursuits and exploits that had characterized the bulk of his reign. Solomon had thrown himself into manifold pleasures, devoted himself to work, and sought out the wisdom of the sharpest minds. But now, looking back on it all with the prospect of a shrinking kingdom looming for his son, Solomon called all of it meaningless. Instead, Solomon taught that every human being—man or woman, king or subject—should have one primary pursuit. He wrote:

> "The conclusion, when all has been heard, is: fear God and keep His commandments, because this applies to every person. For God will bring every act to judgment, everything which is hidden, whether it is good or evil." (Ecclesiastes 12:13–14)

Place yourself in Solomon's shoes for a moment. Think about what Solomon knew—his son was walking into a job that would consume the rest of his life and at which he was going to be a failure. Solomon knew he bore responsibility for setting his son on this path. The guilt must have been overwhelming. Solomon also knew that with his selfish pursuits he personally had not honored or "feared" God. As a result, Solomon knew he had failed to live a life of obedience.

Solomon's last words clearly articulate God's will for all people. Fleeting pleasure, the demanding job, and the penetrating truth are not worth a life lived without concern for the Lord. God wants us to order our lives in light of Him—obeying His commands, which we find throughout His Word. When the apostle James called caring for the helpless of society true religion, we should make sure to take part in such work (James 1:27). When the prophet Amos pronounced judgment on God's people for their taking advantage of the needy, we need to check our pride and find ways to counteract such deeds. When Jesus called us to love our neighbor, we need to seek out opportunities to show the people around us that we are committed to their well-being. Such deeds characterize the obedient Christian.

Solomon's last words also indicate that obedience is not a one-time event but rather a life-long pursuit. Such consistent obedience doesn't come naturally to us. But God has sent us a Helper, the Holy Spirit, who empowers believers to make obedience a habit. Believers hope to see our lives transformed by the Spirit so that we might live according to God's design for us. On a practical level, when we live in deference to God, we will naturally order our lives around God's commands for us. When we do those two things, we show ourselves as people who will avoid the dark side of Solomon's stark conclusion: God will judge every one of our acts, both good and evil.

— *John Adair*

SIMEON'S PATIENCE

"Behold, this Child is appointed for the fall and rise of many in Israel, and for a sign to be opposed — and a sword will pierce even your own soul — to the end that thoughts from many hearts may be revealed."

— Luke 2:34–35

In a world of microwaves and text messages, instant gratification is a way of life. Why wait when we don't have to? Patience may be a virtue, but the busy lives we lead just don't leave any room for waiting. We wake in the morning, zip through the coffee shop drive thru, zoom to work, rush through meetings, skip lunch, fly home, hurry to extracurricular activities, hit the local fast-food restaurant, arrive home late, and crash in our beds. When life moves a million miles a second, we simply don't have time to slow down and wait for anything. Or do we?

Many of us live hurried spiritual lives too. With schedules like ours, how can we take the time to pray, read God's Word, meditate on His promises, and listen to Him? So we read a few verses as we wait for our coffee, shoot off a quick prayer, and we're on our way. But God asks His children to slow down and patiently wait for Him. If we don't have time, maybe we should reevaluate our priorities.

Luke 2:25–35 tells us about Simeon, a man who showed supernatural patience as he waited for the arrival of the Messiah. Each day Simeon watched for Messiah, trusting that one day he would meet Him, just as God had promised (Luke 2:26). And after a lifetime of anticipation, Simeon was finally allowed to meet the holy Child.

Simeon was a devout Jew on whom the Holy Spirit had rested. Unlike many Jews of that day who concerned themselves with legalism and retaining their power in the Roman society, Simeon was part of the believing remnant of Israel who prayed for Messiah to come and bring forgiveness to all people. Day in and day out, Simeon anticipated God's Messiah. Finally, one day the Holy Spirit led Simeon to the temple courts where he met Mary and Joseph as they brought baby Jesus to dedicate Him to the Lord.

As Simeon's eyes met Jesus's, Simeon recognized the salvation he had so patiently looked for. Having met the Messiah face to face, Simeon could die at peace with the God who had revealed His salvation. Simeon praised God for sending His Servant who would light the way for both Jews and Gentiles. Simeon had been waiting for God to fulfill the words of Isaiah the prophet, who proclaimed the good news of a savior through whom God would restore and comfort Israel and all nations (Isaiah 52:7–10). Simeon rejoiced with the psalmist who said:

> He has remembered
> His lovingkindness
> and His faithfulness
> to the house of Israel;
>
> All the ends of
> the earth have seen
> the salvation of our
> God. (Psalm 98:3)

Then Simeon blessed the family, and with his last words, Simeon foretold the divisive ministry of Jesus and the painful loss Mary would endure as her Son hung on the cross. He said: "Behold, this Child is appointed for the fall and rise of many in Israel, and for a sign to be opposed—and a sword will pierce even your own soul—to the end that thoughts from many hearts may be revealed" (Luke 2:34–35). Jesus Christ's message would divide families because often not all family members would believe in Him (12:49–53). And as Simeon prophesied, Messiah's unexpected and humiliating death on the cross would be a stumbling block to many Jews and Gentiles (Isaiah 8:15; 1 Corinthians 1:22–24).

Simeon's patience paid off because he received the object of his hope. But what about those who didn't? Abraham, Isaac, Jacob, Moses, and others knew about God's promise of restoration through the Messiah, but they never received the object of this promise. Even still, with faith, hope, and amazing patience they looked forward to the day when Jesus Christ would come (Hebrews 11:13–16, 39–40). God allowed Simeon to see the hope the patriarchs longed for.

Simeon waited his whole life for the Messiah and trusted in God's promise that the Christ would come in Simeon's lifetime. So with laser focus, Simeon kept his eyes fixed on God's faithful character and waited. But as Simeon waited, he didn't stop moving. Patience doesn't equal inactivity. Simeon kept serving the Lord, praying that God would fulfill His promise, and living every day with hope. And Simeon no doubt shared with others his hope in Messiah's advent.

Having met the Messiah face to face, Simeon could die at peace with the God who had revealed His salvation.

If patience marks the life of a child of God, shouldn't we slow down and incorporate this virtue into our lives? Our willingness to wait for the Lord's perfect timing reveals whether or not we truly trust Him. In order to wait patiently for God to answer our prayers and fulfill His promises, we have to keep our eyes fixed on Him.

We must ask ourselves: Does patience mark my life? When I pray, do I expect God to answer my prayers immediately and then get mad when He doesn't? The Lord is eternal, and so is His perspective. He sees all of history at once. Yesterday, today, and tomorrow are the same to Him. When we develop an eternal perspective, patience will begin to infiltrate our thoughts and actions. So let's pray with faith and patiently wait on the Lord's perfect timing (Psalm 40:1–3). And as we wait for the Lord to answer our prayers and fulfill His promises, we must keep moving, keep serving Him, and keep sharing about the God who patiently waits for all people to believe in Him (2 Peter 3:9).

— *Malia Rodriguez*

JUDAS'S SORROW

"I have sinned by betraying

innocent blood."...And

he threw the pieces of silver

into the temple sanctuary

and departed; and he went

away and hanged himself.

—Matthew 27:4–5

is name is a byword for betrayal. But it never began that way.

"Judas" is the Greek form for the Hebrew name Judah — a common designation in Israel. In fact, Judas wasn't the only one of the twelve disciples with that name, but he made it infamous.

Judas's treacherous betrayal came as a complete shock to all who knew him. On the surface, he appeared as dedicated as all the other apostles. Chosen by Jesus. Worker of miracles. Even entrusted as treasurer. So when Jesus foretold His own betrayal at the Last Supper, no disciple at the table pointed and said, "Aha, Judas! I knew there was something about you!" The whole group remained clueless. Each one, in fact, asked, "Surely not I, Lord?"

(Matthew 26:22). Strangely, even Judas asked.

From the human perspective, Judas's motive for betrayal may have had its roots in the love of money (John 12:6). Pure greed. But from the spiritual perspective, the inspirational source is clear: Satan influenced Judas to betray Jesus (Luke 22:3–4).

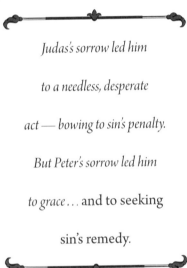

Judas's sorrow led him

to a needless, desperate

act — bowing to sin's penalty.

But Peter's sorrow led him

to grace… and to seeking

sin's remedy.

Judas descended from the Upper Room in the blackness of night in order to guide the authorities to Jesus. They found the Master in the garden of Gethsemane, and Judas arranged a sign to identify which man to arrest.

A kiss of greeting.

Judas approached Jesus in the dark grove and gave his false-hearted kiss of respect. "Greetings, Rabbi," he blathered — even his words betrayed his actions. This pretentious kiss of greeting also served as an unwitting farewell.

True, no one expected Judas's betrayal. No one but Jesus. The Lord knew from the beginning who would betray Him (John 6:64). Jesus's response to the disingenuous salutation exposed Judas's intent.

"Judas, are you betraying the Son of Man with a kiss?" (Luke 22:48). Jesus's last words to Judas would echo in his ears for eternity.

After Judas discovered that Jesus faced death, "he felt remorse and returned the thirty pieces of silver to the chief priests and elders, saying, 'I have sinned by betraying innocent blood'" (Matthew 27:3–4). After hurling the lucre into the temple, Judas selected a spot and hanged himself.

Some have mused whether or not Judas ever truly believed in Jesus. Although God's grace is big enough to have forgiven Judas, it seems unlikely that the betrayer's "remorse" resulted in repentance. Several factors make this clear.

First, Jesus namelessly called Judas a "devil" (John 6:70) and said it would be better for him had he not been born (Mark 14:21). In referring to the disciples, Jesus told the Father, "not one of them perished but the son of perdition" (John 17:12).

Second, Jesus told the twelve apostles they would rule over the twelve tribes of Israel in Jesus's kingdom (Matthew 19:28). After Judas's death, the apostles had Judas's position replaced by Matthias. However, they did not replace the apostle James after his death. What's more, Peter implied Judas's condemnation by saying he "turned aside to go to his own place" (Acts 1:25).

Third, the place Judas chose to die may indicate his expectation for eternity. He committed suicide at *Hakeldama*, or "Field of Blood" (1:18–19), located in the Hinnom Valley. This was the first-century landfill that Jesus had used as a metaphor for hell (Mark 9:43).

The infamous betrayer of Jesus always appears last in the gospels' lists of the apostles. Peter always appears first. Interestingly, on the same day that Judas betrayed Jesus, Peter committed a sin just as shocking — he denied Christ. Judas's regret led to suicide, but Peter's regret just occasioned a good cry (and a changed life). What made the difference?

The apostle Paul would later write: "The sorrow that is according to the will of God produces a repentance without regret, leading to salvation, but the sorrow of the world produces death" (2 Corinthians 7:10).

Judas's sorrow led him to a needless, desperate act — bowing to sin's penalty. But Peter's sorrow led him to grace . . . *and to seeking sin's remedy.*

In Judas's final words, "I have sinned," he pronounced his own judgment. His betrayal played a part in Jesus's death which would, amazingly, pay for even Judas's sins. How ironic. How tragic.

Like Judas, like Peter, like all the disciples who deserted Jesus that night — we have a choice regarding where our sorrow will take us. As we face the raw truth of our carnal hearts, our shame and guilt will lead us in one of two directions: toward sin's penalty in death or to sin's remedy in grace.

Thankfully, God intends the pangs of our sorrow to lead us away from our guilt and toward His grace. No sin is too great for God's mercy.

— Wayne Stiles

THE ROBBERS' RESPONSES

"Jesus, remember me when You come in Your kingdom!"

— Luke 23:42

Two thieves hung on either side of God's Son. Along with the Jewish leaders, Roman soldiers, and passersby, they hurled insults at Him. *You healed many and even raised the dead. Why don't you get yourself off the cross? You claim to be the Savior, the promised Messiah, yet you can't save yourself! This is your last chance to prove yourself. And if you do, we will believe! Just show us one more sign . . .*

Even though they had endured flogging and crucifixion, the robbers hanging on Jesus's right and left still had the energy to join the mocking voices (Matthew 27:44). They still didn't get it. These convicted criminals still weren't willing to face their sin and embrace their Savior.

But something changed in the heart of one of the dying convicts. As he listened to Jesus's final words, his doubt turned to faith and his self-righteousness gave way to repentance.

So what did the thieves hear from Jesus? While both thieves stewed in their anger as they faced death for their crimes, they likely yelled curses at their Roman executioners. But Jesus extended grace, acquitted His murderers, and prayed that His Father would forgive them (Luke 23:34). This would have been altogether shocking! Struck by Jesus's mercy and His close fellowship with God, the faithful thief's heart began to soften. Perhaps the believing thief recognized Jesus as the promised Servant who would bear the sins of others and intercede for transgressors (Isaiah 53:12). He stopped mocking Jesus, and he rebuked the unbelieving thief, saying, "Do you not even fear God, since you are under the same sentence of condemnation? And we indeed are suffering justly, for we are receiving what we deserve for our deeds; but this man has done nothing wrong" (Luke 23:40 – 41). The two robbers were paying for their crimes, but Jesus had no sin to pay for.

After watching Jesus extend grace to His persecutors, the believing robber realized that Jesus was different—maybe He truly was the promised Messiah. And if Christ could forgive His executioners, surely He could forgive a robber. So with humility, the thief asked Jesus to remember him — to extend grace — when Christ completed His task and sat down at the Father's right hand (Hebrews 1:3).

Repeatedly in His ministry, Jesus had taught that salvation is God's gift and faith is our obedient response. So, with his dying breath, one robber proclaimed his faith: "Jesus, remember me when You come in Your kingdom!" (Luke 23:42). Jesus's acceptance of the last words of the believing thief teaches us that faith, not works, reconciles us with God. And this "deathbed conversion" is not the exception to the rule — it *is* the rule.

But both robbers heard Jesus Christ's words of forgiveness. Why did only one believe? Why did the other criminal use his dying words to declare his unbelief, saying with mockery and scorn, "Are You not the Christ? Save Yourself and us!" (Luke 23:39).

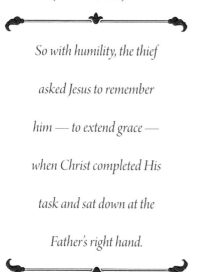

So with humility, the thief

asked Jesus to remember

him — to extend grace —

when Christ completed His

task and sat down at the

Father's right hand.

Pride is the root of unbelief. The thief who didn't believe may not have been willing to admit his depravity and let go of the desire to justify himself. Still today, with a clenched fist raised at heaven, many people refuse to acknowledge their sin and their need for a savior. Many people think they are basically good. But a perfect God demands perfection, which

is possible only through faith in Christ (John 14:6).

All human beings are like these two thieves—deserving of death for our rebellion against God. Many of us Christians were liars, thieves, idolaters, even murderers until God saved us (1 Corinthians 6:9–11). Through Christ, God extended grace and promised us eternal fellowship with Him. Through trials, blessing, and the slow thaw of our ice-cold hearts, God softened us to the gospel. And like one of the thieves, through the power of the Holy Spirit, we believed.

Every aspect of salvation is God's work. Faith is the gift of God, and nothing can separate believers from God's love (Romans 8:38–39; Ephesians 2:8–9). Sanctification is accomplished by means of the Spirit, not by human works (Romans 8:1–11). And glorification will occur when God raises us from the dead, removes our sin nature, and clothes us with glorified bodies (John 6:37–40; 1 Corinthians 15:51–57). If you'd like to learn more about the concepts presented here, see "How to Begin a Relationship with God" at the back of this book. *None* of this happens by will power or human intellect, so pride has no place in the life of a believer.

So, now what? God doesn't want us to carry on our shoulders the load of our eternal destiny. He wants us to know that His love does not depend on our works (Romans 5:8–10). Though obedience leads to closer fellowship with the Lord, obedience doesn't define God's love. No matter what crimes we've committed, the Lord waits with open arms and unlimited grace for believers and unbelievers to come to Him.

— *Malia Rodriguez*

JESUS'S ACCOMPLISHMENT

"Father, into Your hands

I commit My spirit."

—Luke 23:46

Jesus Christ, the God-Man, stands at the center of Christian faith. We cling to Jesus because He opens the way to the Father for all of us, who have been rebellious. He granted us unfettered access to the Father by means of His death and resurrection. In the final hours of Jesus's life, some of the most significant moments in all of human history, Jesus spoke. He uttered His final words while hanging from that torturous cross, a six-hour ordeal during which the Lord made seven separate statements that have been recorded in the gospels. These seven statements, traditionally ordered, offer a poignant reflection on the nature and work of Jesus, as well as relationships, loneliness, and faith.

"Father, forgive them; for they do not know what they are doing" (Luke 23:34).

When Jesus spoke these words, He focused on the actions of those who nailed Him to the cross, those who spat upon Him, and those who called for His execution. The Lord's forgiveness was spread wide and offered to many, even to those responsible for such great evil. Many of us feel acutely the ways we have failed God and have wallowed in unrighteous living. If Jesus forgave those who crucified Him, can He not also forgive us?

"Truly I say to you, today you shall be with Me in Paradise" (Luke 23:43). While many responded to Jesus's offer of forgiveness with sneering, mocking, and abusive words, one of the thieves crucified that day defended Jesus and expressed his faith in Jesus's kingdom. In response to Jesus's offer of forgiveness, this thief opened himself to God and received salvation. This scene gives us a miniature picture of the world as it remains today: the call for forgiveness goes out to all, but only a few come to Jesus in faith, while the rest of humanity persists in hatred, rejection, and rebellion.

"Woman, behold, your son! . . . Behold, your mother!" (John 19:26–27). When the Roman soldiers nailed Jesus to the cross, it left a void in the world. His followers would now have to carry on without His bodily presence. Jesus asked His mother and His dear friend to care for each other. In this statement, Jesus reminds us that entering into a relationship of faith with God also involves entering into relationships with other believers. God has given us the body of Christ, His church, to fill the void of fellowship as we await Jesus's return.

"My God, My God, why have You forsaken Me?" (Matthew 27:46). While God's people would experience the warmth of genuine fellowship with one another, Jesus found Himself in a much different place at His moment of greatest sacrifice. The Lord received numerous physical wounds from beatings and from the crucifixion itself, but His greatest wound came when He entered spiritual death — separation from the Father — as payment for our sins. Jesus's loneliness in that moment reminds us of the high cost of a life devoted to sacrifice. Our response to such a gift should be one of gratitude.

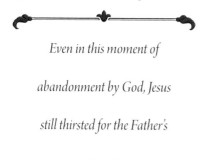

Even in this moment of abandonment by God, Jesus still thirsted for the Father's presence.

"I am thirsty" (John 19:28). Alone on the cross, with virtually all of His disciples having left Him and only a few weak and scattered followers among the throngs of those who wanted His head, Jesus found Himself in distress. He who was the source of "living water" (7:37–39) now asked for a drink, a reality that only serves to heighten the tragedy of the moment. John's gospel links Jesus's request to Old Testament Scripture that includes the Messiah's suffering with a thirst (Psalm 22:15; 69:21). The soldiers gave Jesus wine on a hyssop branch. This is the final time in Scripture that hyssop is mentioned; the first time was at the first Passover — when a lamb

died to save the firstborn of Israel. All of our lives should be lived in honor of God's Word, just as Jesus saw the connection between His thirst and Scripture.

"It is finished!" (John 19:30). Jesus spoke these words when He received the sour wine. He understood that, having fulfilled all prophecy and, therefore, His mission from the Father, He had completed His work on earth. The phrasing in John's gospel carries the sense that Jesus recognized He had accomplished a great work. The perfect sacrifice had been made. This statement by Jesus marks a moment of triumph after a lifetime of teaching, sacrificing, and suffering. What kind of goal do we see ourselves working toward? When death comes for us, will we be able to echo these words of Jesus? Will our work — the work that God created us to do — have been accomplished?

"Father, into Your hands I commit My spirit" (Luke 23:46). This final statement of Jesus on the cross, comprising His true last words, indicates an imminent reunion with the Father. After the terrifying moments of forsaken darkness that Jesus experienced on the cross, He still believed. Jesus continued to trust that the Father would welcome Him back now that the work was complete. This stunning celebration of deep and abiding faith can speak even to the hardest of hearts among us. None of us experience a trial on the level of Jesus, the Son of God forsaken by the Father. But we experience trials similar to the one our Lord experienced. In light of His example, let us strive to awaken each day with the goal to trust in the Father's mercy. The Father rescued Jesus, the forsaken One. How much more will He do for us whom He has forgiven?

— *John Adair*

SAPPHIRA'S FIB

She said, "Yes, that was the price." Then Peter said to her, "Why is it that you have agreed together to put the Spirit of the Lord to the test?"

—Acts 5:8–9

Sapphira and Ananias lied . . . to God, to Peter, and to the church, and they paid a dear price for it.

In the early days, members of the body of believers in Christ cared for one another in communal accord. When the church was in need, various members would sell their property and take the proceeds to the apostles, who would then allocate the funds to care for the needy (Acts 4:32, 34–35). Two members of this body of Christ-followers — husband and wife Ananias and Sapphira — sold a piece of their property and chose to secretly keep for themselves a portion of the proceeds (5:1–2).

Whether tacitly or explicitly, they committed to donate the full proceeds, but they failed to do so; then they gave the false impression to the community that they had. Still, Ananias and Sapphira hadn't really hurt anyone by holding back a cut from the sale of their land — land that had been their own possession, after all! No harm, no foul, right? Who would have ever known they didn't give the full amount to the church? Probably, no one.

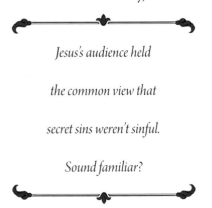

Jesus's audience held

the common view that

secret sins weren't sinful.

Sound familiar?

But God knew, and through the intervention of the Holy Spirit, the apostle Peter knew too. Peter pointed out Ananias and Sapphira's evil intent. Both had an opportunity to repent. Both chose to lie. And God brought the ultimate discipline upon them: immediate death.

We might think: *That's so unfair! Why would God take someone's life because of a simple fib?*

That's harsh! Ananias and Sapphira just failed to disclose all the facts. We've all withheld certain information to make ourselves look better. What's the big deal?

A destructive mind-set ran rampant among the people in those days, especially among the Pharisees — the notion that exhibiting godliness through public acts of contrition or generosity mattered more than actually being godly. Praying loudly in public, making a show of fasting, and giving money in full view of peers were popular practices. Jesus spoke strongly against such false piety: "You [Pharisees] are those who justify yourselves in the sight of men, but God knows your hearts; for that which is highly esteemed among men is detestable in the sight of God" (Luke 16:15).

Likewise, Peter admonished Ananias and Sapphira: "You have not lied to men but to God" (Acts 5:4). This idea harkened back to Jesus's paradigm-shifting revelation atop the Mount of Beatitudes that inward, private sin is no less sinful than outward, public sin. "You have heard that it was said, 'You shall not commit adultery'; but I say to you that everyone who looks at a woman with lust for her has already committed adultery with her in his heart" (Matthew 5:27–28).

Jesus's audience held the common view that secret sins weren't sinful. Sound familiar? Sound like Ananias and Sapphira? Sound like us?

Yelling profanities in the privacy of your vehicle at the driver in the car in front of you who rudely cut you off is just as offensive to God as screaming profanities out the window so the other person can hear you. Again, Jesus said in His Sermon on the Mount: "But I say, if you are even angry with someone, you are subject to judgment! . . . And if you curse someone, you are in danger of the fires of hell (5:22 NLT). First Samuel 16:7 reminds us that the Lord does not see as mortals see; they look at the outward appearance, but the Lord looks at the heart.

Humans rank sin, considering some sins to be terrible and others to be tolerable. But to God, sin is sin no matter how great or small—no matter how secret or public. All sin is inexcusable. Why? Because God is holy (Leviticus 11:44–45; 19:2; 1 Samuel 2:2). He's so holy that anything — *anything* — unholy is abhorrent to Him. He cannot and will not tolerate unholiness. And because God is intolerant to sin, sin separates us from Him, bringing spiritual death to the sinner.

Thankfully, death is not the end of the story. Because God loves His creation, He has provided a way for His people to avoid the eternal death that sin causes. Through the precious price paid via His life, death, and resurrection, Jesus Christ saves believers from the punishment their sins deserve. To learn more about how Jesus Christ can bring a person from eternal death to eternal life, see "How to Begin a Relationship with God" at the end of this book.

As we consider the grave account of Ananias and Sapphira,

we must ask searching questions of ourselves: Do I hold on to a private, secret sin? Do I rationalize, thinking that because my sin is secret, it can't hurt anyone? Do I think it can't hurt *me*? Do I hold back snippets of truth to make myself appear more holy? Do I deny truth to avoid godly admonitions? If we can answer yes to any of those, we must confess our sin to God immediately and commit to turn from it. Otherwise, God — as a loving Father — will exact discipline on us, His children (Hebrews 12:7–8).

We aren't told the last words of Ananias, but Sapphira's speak for both of them. In answer to Peter's question about the land sale, she responded, "Yes, that was the price" (Acts 5:8). What a fitting word: *price*. Sapphira lied about the price of the land she sold . . . and then she paid the ultimate price for lying: her life.

— *Jim Craft*

STEPHEN'S CROSS

Then falling on his knees, he cried out with a loud voice, "Lord, do not hold this sin against them!" Having said this, he fell asleep.

— Acts 7:60

Many believers know him as the first Christian martyr. Stephen was a man who extended the kind of grace we don't see very often today and the kind of courage we don't think we could ever muster. Besides, does God really expect everyday believers like us to forgive others with the extravagant grace that Stephen showed? He was a heroic man, but we're just normal Christians. And we probably won't be killed for our faith, so we won't have the opportunity to forgive an offender with our dying breath.

But sometimes it may be just as hard to forgive others with our living breath.

Stephen's last words, "Lord, do not hold this sin against them!" echo some of Jesus Christ's dying words. While Jesus hung on the cross, bearing on His shoulders the full weight of the world's sin, Jesus asked His Father to forgive His murderers because they didn't fully understand their actions (Luke 23:34).

So how did Stephen, a man only mentioned a few times in the New Testament, develop such a Christlike character? How could he, while enduring a painful execution, extend forgiveness to his killers?

In Acts 6, we learn a little bit about the strength of Stephen. The apostles faced the first church conflict when the Hellenists claimed that their widows had been discriminated against in the daily distribution of food (Acts 6:1). While the Hebrew widows received from the church everything they needed to survive, the Hellenistic widows were being left out. So the apostles selected seven men "of good reputation, full of the Spirit and of wisdom," to ensure that everyone received an equal share of the church's resources (6:3). This role required grace, sensitivity to the needs of others, love, and not a hint of prejudice. Because of his character, faith, and the evident work of the Spirit in his life, the apostles chose Stephen as one of the seven.

As the young church grew, people started to notice Stephen, who powerfully performed signs and miracles (6:8) and testified that Jesus Christ was the Messiah. Unfortunately, some Jews didn't like what Stephen had to say about Jesus's identity, so they contrived false accusations against Stephen and brought him before the Jewish ruling council (6:9–14). But even in the face of unfounded opposition, grace radiated through Stephen's words, and his face shone with God's love (6:15).

When the high priest demanded a response to the charges of blasphemy, Stephen recounted in the council's hearing the history of Israel. Stephen reminded his audience of God's faithful promise to give Abraham's descendants the land of Canaan. Stephen described God's faithfulness through His provision of Joseph to sustain His people in Egypt and of Moses to deliver them from slavery. Throughout his speech, Stephen highlighted occasions in Israel's history when the people refused to obey God's appointed prophets, the consequences of their disobedience, and the Lord's unlimited forgiveness.

Stephen went on. Not only did the people reject God's prophets of old, they killed the "prophet like [Moses]"—Jesus Christ—who brought ultimate deliverance (Acts 7:37–38). Just as God's people turned against Moses by asking Aaron to fashion idols to worship, the Jews turned against the Lord Jesus in favor of empty religion and political ambition. Because God's people resisted the Holy Spirit's work throughout history to prepare them for the arrival of Messiah, they failed to see Jesus Christ as their long-awaited Messiah (7:51–52).

When Stephen's Jewish audience heard these words, they felt convicted. But instead of repenting, they shook their fists at him in rage (7:54). Miraculously, God opened heaven, and Stephen saw

Jesus standing at the right hand of the Father (7:55–56). The Lord graciously gave Stephen a glimpse into heaven that would sustain him through the agony of being stoned to death. And, knowing that Jesus stood ready to receive Stephen, he forgave his persecutors.

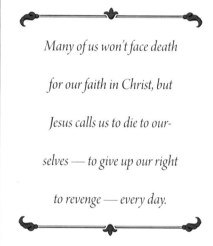

Many of us won't face death for our faith in Christ, but Jesus calls us to die to ourselves — to give up our right to revenge — every day.

When we look at Stephen's last few moments, it's amazing how much they mirror Jesus's last few moments on the cross. But Jesus didn't just speak His last words of extravagant grace so that martyrs like Stephen could repeat them. Jesus spoke His words of ultimate forgiveness so that believers' lives would display the forgiveness He extended and modeled.

Many of us won't face death for our faith in Christ, but Jesus calls us to die to ourselves—to give up our right to revenge—every day. He beckons us to pick up our metaphorical crosses and follow Him (Matthew 16:24; Mark 8:34; Luke 9:23). And part of following Jesus in this way includes forgiving others when we have been wronged, hurt, and deeply offended. Pride encourages us to hold on to bitterness, to defend our right to retribution, and to take justice into our own hands. But Jesus calls us to practice humility, forgive easily, and leave vengeance to the Lord (Romans 12:19).

What offenses have we held on to, refusing to trust the Lord to make things right? As we learn to forgive others, let's follow Stephen's example as he looked intently at Jesus Christ, who stood in triumph over sin and death. Like Stephen, let's allow the Holy Spirit to fill and control us so we can extend forgiveness even for the most horrible wrongs committed against us. And let's trust that at the end of time, Jesus will return to deal with all sin. Though we may at times be victims of injustice, the grace we show will point others to God's perfect forgiveness.

— *Malia Rodriguez*

PAUL'S OFFERING

For I am already being poured out as a drink offering, and the time of my departure has come.

—2 Timothy 4:6

As he sat in his underground prison cell, wishing he had a warm coat and his favorite books, Paul reflected on his life. All the memories, the pain and joy, the reward and sacrifice, flooded his mind. So Paul picked up his quill and wrote one final letter to Timothy, his beloved son in the faith (2 Timothy 1:2). As his hand followed the thoughts in his mind, one word kept coming back—*sacrifice*. That's what it would take for Timothy to stay the course and to fulfill the pastoral calling God had given him. And that's what it will take for all Christians to carry out the ministry God has given each of us.

In his final letter, the worn and aged apostle to the Gentiles charged his young protégé to preach God's Word without compromise. The apostle Paul warned Timothy that the day would come when people would reject sound biblical doctrine in favor of myths. While the Bible teaches self-denial, obedience, and humility, our human nature clamors for messages that support indulgence, self-determination, and fame. But many don't realize that true life comes by way of death, and honor comes through sacrifice.

And the apostle Paul poured out his life as an offering like few others have.

So what made Paul, the man who once persecuted Christians, so willing to sacrifice and even die for the Lord he used to hate? Paul constantly looked back to his Damascus road conversion experience and Jesus Christ's clear call to take the gospel to the Gentiles. And Paul always looked forward to the victorious crown awaiting him in Christ's presence.

We first meet Paul as Saul in Acts 7:58 as he guarded the robes of the men stoning Stephen. Saul, who was born in Tarsus, reared in Jerusalem, and educated under Gamaliel in the strictest

sect of Judaism, was a rising star among the Pharisees (Acts 22:3; 26:4–5). Brilliant and zealous, Saul persecuted Christians with vigor.

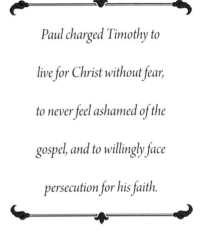

Paul charged Timothy to live for Christ without fear, to never feel ashamed of the gospel, and to willingly face persecution for his faith.

But as Saul traveled to Damascus to terrorize Christians, Jesus appeared to him and redirected his entire life (9:1–30). Jesus humbled Saul, whose name means "the asked for one," and he began to be called Paul, which means "small." Paul would have to remain small — and the Lord huge — in order for Paul to endure the path of sacrifice that God had set out for him.

After his conversion, humility, grace, and self-denying love characterized Paul's ministry. Paul lived by his words in Galatians 2:20: "I have been crucified with Christ; and it is no longer I who live, but Christ lives in me; and the life which I now live in the flesh I live by faith in the Son of God, who loved me and gave Himself up for me." It's no wonder that, after giving his pastoral charge to Timothy, Paul modeled ultimate sacrifice by giving his life for Christ. The book of 2 Timothy represents Paul's famous last words.

In 2 Timothy chapter 1, Paul charged Timothy to live for Christ without fear, to never feel ashamed of the gospel, and to willingly face persecution for his faith (2 Timothy 1:8). And in chapter 2, Paul outlined the requirements for faithful service, which demanded that Timothy have an eternal perspective, not a temporal focus. That would allow Timothy to treat life as a marathon that could be won only through righteous living and self-denial (2:22–26).

In 2 Timothy 3, Paul reminded Timothy that God allows difficulty to befall His children in order to develop their endurance and faith (3:10–12). And in chapter 4, Paul charged Timothy to preach the Word clearly and without compromise (4:1–2). Paul commanded Timothy to teach sound doctrine in order to please the Lord (4:3–4), to work as an evangelist, to expect trials, and to fulfill the ministry that God had given him (4:5).

As Paul shared his hard-earned wisdom with Timothy, he anticipated one final act of faith. Paul knew that any day the Roman executioner would enter his prison cell and lead him to his death. But Paul was ready — he had always viewed his life as an ever-flowing drink offering to the Lord: "For I am already being poured out as a drink offering, and the time of my departure has come" (4:6).

In the Old Testament, God commanded His people to pour onto the altar offerings of strong, undiluted wine (Numbers 28:7). The Israelites made these drink offerings to the Lord to remember His provision of the Promised Land and to thank Him for the rest and joy He had given them. Offerings and sacrifices pointed forward to the perfect, sinless sacrifice of Jesus Christ.

So what characterizes our lives as Christians? Are we actively sacrificing or relinquishing our gifts, resources, and time to the Lord for His use? Or are we holding on to these things, thinking that carefully controlling them will bring us security and happiness? Let's learn from the apostle Paul, whose eyes were fixed on the reward awaiting him in heaven (2 Timothy 4:8). Out of gratitude for the Lord's grace in our lives, let's fulfill the calling and the ministry He has given us and stay true to the truth in His Word (4:5–7). And let's present ourselves, body and soul, to the Lord as living sacrifices for His use (Romans 12:1–2). Like Paul, we will start experiencing true joy and purpose through our willing sacrifice.

— *Malia Rodriguez*

PETER'S REMINDER

Birthdays. Anniversaries. National holidays. Christmas. These special days circle around each year to do more than remind us we were born or that we got married or we live in our country or it's time to go shopping. These celebrations prompt us to think *about* a person and *about* marriage and *about* patriotism and *about* the incarnation. These special days urge us to stop and consider life's essentials—those important things we might otherwise neglect, or worse, forget.

The spiritual life has its cues as well. In fact, God built memory triggers into His plan for His people. The annual Passover feast reminded the Hebrews of their redemption by God (Exodus 12:25–27). Moses commanded them to listen to

Scripture read aloud every seven years (Deuteronomy 31:10–11). The Lord Jesus, the night before He died, instituted a recurring ordinance for the church—Communion, or the Lord's Supper—to commemorate His death on our behalf (Luke 22:19). The apostle Paul wrote the Philippians the "same things again" as a safeguard for them (Philippians 3:1). Repetition is woven into the fiber of God's intentions.

Remember that

God's Word is our only

guide for life.

At the end of the apostle Peter's life, he picked up his quill and scratched out a short letter, his second epistle, which represents his last words. As Peter pressed the nib to the parchment, one theme continued to recur: the need for reminders of spiritual truths (2 Peter 1:9–15; 3:1–2). Maybe it was the recurring Jewish feasts and festivals Peter had celebrated all his life. Or perhaps it was the many Communion meals he had eaten. Or maybe Peter simply had a seasoned understanding of the forgetfulness of human nature. Whatever the reason, Peter's purpose in his letter is clear:

> This is now, beloved, the second letter I am writing to you in which I am stirring up your sincere mind by way of reminder, that you should remember the words spoken beforehand by the holy prophets and the commandment of the Lord and Savior spoken by your apostles.
> (2 Peter 3:1–2)

No doubt, Peter had learned a lot about which he could have written them. Hardly the bumbling fisherman who walked with Jesus for three years during His earthly ministry, Peter had now lived more than three decades as an apostle of Jesus. His knowledge and faith had matured beyond the basics. But instead of taking his readers to the next level theologically, the aged apostle reaffirmed the importance of what they already knew (2 Peter 1:12). Peter's time was short: "The laying aside of my earthly dwelling is imminent," he wrote; therefore, "I will also be diligent that at any time after my departure you will be able to call these things to mind" (1:14–15).

Peter's letter zeroes in on the importance of continued exposure to Scripture—both the Old Testament ("the words spoken beforehand by the holy prophets") and in the New Testament ("the commandment of the Lord and Savior spoken by your apostles"). The reasons for these reminders are at least three, and the principles they offer are timeless.

First, remember that God is our only source of truth. Peter's day had its mystics and preachers of relative truth, just as ours does. So Peter assured them that he and the other apostles didn't concoct the stories they told about Jesus: "We did not follow cleverly devised tales when we made known to you the power

and coming of our Lord Jesus Christ, but we were eyewitnesses of His majesty" (1:16). They saw Jesus, His miracles, His death and resurrection. Specifically, Peter had witnessed firsthand the Lord's majesty on the Mount of Transfiguration where he heard the Father's voice affirm: "This is My beloved Son with whom I am well-pleased" (1:17–18; see also Matthew 17:1–8). The basis of truth isn't opinion or reason—but revelation from God.

Second, remember that God's Word is our only guide for life. Anybody can claim to have a message from God. Therefore, Peter pointed his readers back to the Bible as their guide, comparing God's Word to a lamp that guides in the darkness (2 Peter 1:19; see also Psalm 119:105). It shows us which way to go. It exposes truth the darkness hides. Peter referred to the Bible as God's "precious and magnificent promises, [given] so that by them you may become partakers of the divine nature" (2 Peter 1:4).

Third, remember that the Word of God originated with

God. This may seem basic, but the basics are the most important; that's why Peter repeated them. "No prophecy was ever made by an act of human will, but men moved by the Holy Spirit spoke from God" (2 Peter 1:21). In our day as well, the divine inspiration of Scripture undergirds everything the Bible teaches. Undermine Scripture, and our faith collapses. Reiterate it, and we stay strong. God's Word came from God.

Not long after Peter put down his pen, Jesus's words about how Peter would die came true (John 21:18–19). It is traditionally believed that the apostle was crucified upside down in Rome for the faith he proclaimed. Peter's final words bear the marks of one who did more than make claims. He was one who believed what he saw, wrote reminders of essential truths, and then died faithful to what he had written.

Peter was right. Only by continually remembering what we already know can we remain willing to live and to die for those essential truths.

— *Wayne Stiles*

JOHN'S EXPECTATION

Come, Lord Jesus.

—Revelation 22:20

Preaching a message that God's kingdom was at hand, Jesus called a fisherman named John to follow Him (Mark 1:14–20). As a young disciple, John walked in the footsteps of this great visionary. Jesus's message of inaugurating a perfect kingdom on earth created an expectation of redemption that would become, for John, the defining narrative of his life.

We see glimpses of hope for the future throughout John's life and experiences with Jesus. John grew up in a fisherman's family. His father, Zebedee, plied his trade on the waters of the Sea of Galilee. When Jesus first approached this son of Zebedee, the young man was in a boat near the shoreline mending nets with his brother, James. As Jesus approached and called him, John was engaged in the work of restoration, renewing nets that had been worn down. The call of Jesus introduced to John a new sort of restorative work, attending to the spiritual lives of broken people.

Some time later, as Jesus and the disciples ministered along the Sea of Galilee, a synagogue official named Jairus fell at Jesus's feet and implored the teacher to heal his gravely ill daughter. Jesus agreed and followed Jairus, but the large crowd caused a delay so long that messengers came from Jairus's house announcing the death of his daughter. Jesus went to the house anyway, taking only three disciples with Him, John among them. John stood by the bedside as Jesus commanded the dead girl to rise. Amazingly, she did (Mark 5:41–42). Such an incident revealed to John that, with Jesus, life would triumph over death.

The foreshadowing of the kingdom during John's time as a disciple was unmistakable on another occasion as well (Matthew 16:28–17:13). The Lord had just finished teaching the disciples that some of them would see Him coming in His kingdom. Six days later, Jesus fulfilled this promise when He took Peter, James, and John up the side of a mountain. While in this secluded place, Jesus was transfigured before the three apostles. Jesus's face shone like the sun and His garments were bright white. The three men watched as Jesus spoke with Moses and Elijah—still alive even though they had died long before. This vision of the future kingdom on a small scale very nearly overwhelmed the apostles. And when the Father spoke His approval onto the scene, John and the other disciples fell to the ground in fear. Jesus helped them up, soothed their fears, and taught them that "Elijah" would come to "restore all things" (17:11)—a reference to the ministry of John the Baptist. Again the apostle John found himself trying to understand the coming kingdom, life after death, and the restoration of all things.

Yet another incident in the apostle John's life stands out for its focus on the future. Once Jesus and the disciples had arrived in

Jerusalem for their final time together, John and a small group of disciples sat with Jesus on the Mount of Olives, overlooking the city. Their questions to Jesus revolved around events in the future. Jesus told them about the coming wrath of God, the return of the Son of Man (Himself), and the need for the disciples to stay on the alert (Matthew 24; Mark 13). The kingdom of God would indeed be coming in its fullness, and believers would need to be ready for it.

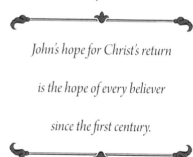

John's hope for Christ's return

is the hope of every believer

since the first century.

These incidents don't encompass the whole of the apostle John's ministry, but they carry a theme that led to the penning of his final words in the book of Revelation. In that oft-ignored book, John recounted the vision he received from God about a future time of wrath to come upon the earth. He also prophesied the return of Jesus and encouraged people to stay ready for the coming of the Lord. John's final words in the book, before the traditional salutation, sum up his concern: "Come, Lord Jesus" (Revelation 22:20). John had lived a long life. He had out-lived all the other apostles, and he sat in exile on the stony island of Patmos. Alone with only the hope of God's good kingdom to come, John yearned for the coming of the Lord.

John's hope for Christ's return is the hope of every believer since the first century. We, too, yearn for the return of Christ because we, too, yearn to see the restoration of all things. God has promised that He intends to restore the earth to its former glory—and John's book of Revelation shows us this in its final two chapters. The destructive effects of sin will be burned away, and the New Heaven and the New Earth will sparkle with the glory of God. Of course, that restored creation will also include us. God means to make human beings new as well, so that we might live and work and worship on earth as He intended, for all eternity. As the dirt and the grime of life threaten our joy and compromise our purity, let us all fix our eyes on God's Son, who will deliver a new and better world unto us. Come, Lord Jesus!

— *John Adair*

HOW TO BEGIN A RELATIONSHIP WITH GOD

Success and failure mark our lives. Thankfully, God has included in His Word real stories of real people in order to point all people toward their need for restoration and relationship with Him. Through the good news found in the Bible, the Lord changes lives and breathes eternal life into ailing souls. From Genesis to Revelation, God reveals four essential truths we must accept and apply if we are to find the life-transforming remedy He offers us. Let's look at these four truths in detail.

Our Spiritual Condition: Totally Depraved

The first truth is rather personal. One look in the mirror of Scripture, and our human condition becomes painfully clear:

"There is none righteous, not even one;
There is none who understands,
There is none who seeks for God;
All have turned aside, together they have become useless;
There is none who does good,
There is not even one." (Romans 3:10–12)

We are all sinners through and through—totally depraved. Now, that doesn't mean we've committed every atrocity known to humankind. We're not as *bad* as we can be, just as *bad off* as we can be. Sin colors all our thoughts, motives, words, and actions.

If you've been around a while, you likely already believe it. Look around. Everything around us bears the smudge marks of our sinful nature. Despite our best efforts to create a perfect world, crime statistics continue to soar, divorce rates keep climbing, and families keep crumbling.

Something has gone terribly wrong in our society and in ourselves—something deadly. Contrary to how the world would repackage it, "me-first" living doesn't equal rugged individuality and freedom; it equals death. As Paul said in his letter to the Romans, "The wages of sin is death" (Romans 6:23)—our spiritual and physical death that comes from God's righteous judgment of our sin, along with all of the emotional and practical effects of this separation that we experience on a daily basis. This brings us to the second marker: God's character.

God's Character: Infinitely Holy

How can God judge us for a sinful state we were born into? Our total depravity is only half the answer. The other half is God's infinite holiness.

The fact that we know things are not as they should be points us to a standard of goodness beyond ourselves. Our sense of injustice in life on this side of eternity implies a perfect standard of justice beyond our reality. That standard and source is God Himself. And God's standard of holiness contrasts starkly with our sinful condition.

Scripture says that "God is Light, and in Him there is no darkness at all" (1 John 1:5). God is absolutely holy—which creates a problem for us. If He is so pure, how can we who are so impure relate to Him?

Perhaps we could try being better people, try to tilt the balance in favor of our good deeds, or seek out methods for self-improvement. Throughout history, people have attempted to live up to God's standard by keeping the Ten Commandments or living by their own code of ethics. Unfortunately, no one can come close to satisfying the demands of God's law. Romans 3:20 says, "By the works of the Law no flesh will be justified in His sight; for through the Law comes the knowledge of sin."

Our Need: A Substitute

So here we are, sinners by nature and sinners by choice, trying to pull ourselves up by our own bootstraps to attain a relationship with our holy Creator. But every time we try, we fall flat on our faces. We can't live a good enough life to make up for our sin, because God's standard isn't "good enough"—it's *perfection*. And we can't make amends for the offense our sin has created without dying for it.

Who can get us out of this mess?

If someone could live perfectly, honoring God's law, and would bear sin's death penalty for us—in our place—then we would be saved from our predicament. But is there such a person? Thankfully, yes!

Meet your substitute—*Jesus Christ*. He is the One who took death's place for you!

[God] made [Jesus Christ] who knew no sin to be sin on our behalf, so that we might become the righteousness of God in Him. (2 Corinthians 5:21)

God's Provision: A Savior

God rescued us by sending His Son, Jesus, to die on the cross for our sins (1 John 4:9–10). Jesus was fully human and fully divine (John 1:1, 18), a truth that ensures His understanding of our weaknesses, His power to forgive, and His ability to bridge the gap between God and us (Romans 5:6–11). In short, we are "justified as a gift by His grace through the redemption which is in Christ Jesus" (Romans 3:24). Two words in this verse bear further explanation: *justified* and *redemption*.

Justification is God's act of mercy, in which He declares righteous the believing sinners while we are still in our sinning state. Justification doesn't mean that God *makes* us righteous, so that we never sin again, rather that He *declares* us righteous—much like a judge pardons a guilty criminal. Because Jesus took our sin upon Himself and suffered our judgment on the cross, God forgives our debt and proclaims us PARDONED.

Redemption is Christ's act of paying the complete price to release us from sin's bondage. God sent His Son to bear His wrath for all of our sins—past, present, and future (Romans 3:24–26; 2 Corinthians 5:21). In humble obedience, Christ willingly endured the shame of the cross for our sake (Mark 10:45; Romans 5:6–8; Philippians 2:8). Christ's death satisfied God's righteous demands. He no longer holds our sins against us, because His own Son paid the penalty for them. We are freed from the slave market of sin, never to be enslaved again!

Placing Your Faith in Christ

These four truths describe how God has provided a way to Himself through Jesus Christ. Because the price has been paid in full by God, we must respond to His free gift of eternal life in total faith and confidence in Him to save us. We must step forward into the relationship with God that He has prepared for us—not by doing good works or by being a good person, but by coming to Him just as we are and accepting His justification and redemption by faith.

> For by grace you have been saved through faith; and that not of yourselves, it is the gift of God; not as a result of works, so that no one may boast. (Ephesians 2:8–9)

We accept God's gift of salvation simply by placing our faith in Christ alone for the forgiveness of our sins. Would you like to enter a relationship with your Creator by trusting in Christ as your Savior? If so, here's a simple prayer you can use to express your faith:

> *Dear God,*
>
> *I know that my sin has put a barrier between You and me. Thank You for sending Your Son, Jesus, to die in my place. I trust in Jesus alone to forgive my sins, and I accept His gift of eternal life. I ask Jesus to be my personal Savior and the Lord of my life. Thank You. In Jesus's name, amen.*

If you've prayed this prayer or one like it and you wish to find out more about knowing God and His plan for you in the Bible, contact us at Insight for Living Ministries. Our contact information is provided on the following pages.

CHAPTER:VERSE

WE ARE HERE FOR YOU

If you desire to find out more about knowing God and His plan for you in the Bible, contact us. Insight for Living Ministries provides staff pastors who are available for free written correspondence or phone consultation. These seminary-trained and seasoned counselors have years of experience and are well-qualified guides for your spiritual journey.

Please feel welcome to contact your regional office by using the information below.

United States

Insight for Living Ministries
Biblical Counseling Department
Post Office Box 5000
Frisco, Texas 75034-0055
USA
972-473-5097 (Monday through Friday, 8:00 a.m.–5:00 p.m. central time)
www.insight.org/contactapastor

Canada

Insight for Living Canada
Biblical Counseling Department
PO Box 8 Stn A
Abbotsford BC V2T 6Z4
CANADA
1-800-663-7639
info@insightforliving.ca

Australia, New Zealand, and South Pacific

Insight for Living Australia
Pastoral Care
Post Office Box 443
Boronia, VIC 3155
AUSTRALIA
1300 467 444

Guatemala

Apartado Postal 1L
Agencia: Aguilar Batres
01011, Guatemala
GUATEMALA
(502) 4769-7509
infogt@visionparavivir.org

United Kingdom and Europe

Insight for Living United
  Kingdom
Pastoral Care
PO Box 553
Dorking
RH4 9EU
UNITED KINGDOM
0800 787 9364
+44 (0)1306 640156
pastoralcare@insightforliving.org.uk

RESOURCES FOR PROBING FURTHER

The lives of individuals in the pages of Scripture can seem foreign and far removed from our lives today. But as we read their last words, we realize they were human beings with hopes, dreams, and struggles just like ours. And God still speaks powerfully through their lives in the pages of Scripture today. We have compiled a list of resources that will help you dig deeper into the stories and lessons behind these fascinating lives. We hope you will use them to draw closer to our Savior and to gain His wisdom for each new day. Keep in mind as you read these books that we can't always endorse everything a writer or ministry says, so we encourage you to approach these and all other non-biblical resources with wisdom and discernment.

Insight for Living. *Insight's Bible Handbook: Practical Helps for Bible Study*. Plano, Tex.: IFL Publishing House, 2007.

Morgan, G. Campbell. *Life Applications from Every Chapter in the Bible.* Grand Rapids: Fleming H. Revell, 1994.

Swindoll, Charles R. *David: A Man of Passion & Destiny.* Great Lives Series. Nashville: Thomas Nelson, 2008.

Swindoll, Charles R. *Elijah: A Man of Heroism and Humility.* Great Lives Series. Nashville: Word Publishing, 2000.

Swindoll, Charles R. *Fascinating Stories of Forgotten Lives: Rediscovering Some Old Testament Characters.* Great Lives Series. Nashville: Thomas Nelson, 2005.

Swindoll, Charles R. *Jesus: The Greatest Life of All.* Great Lives Series. Nashville: Thomas Nelson, 2008.

Swindoll, Charles R. *Joseph: A Man of Integrity and Forgiveness.* Great Lives Series. Nashville: Thomas Nelson, 1998.

Swindoll, Charles R. *Moses: A Man of Selfless Dedication.* Great Lives Series. Nashville: Thomas Nelson, 1999.

Swindoll, Charles R. *Paul: A Man of Grace and Grit.* Great Lives Series. Nashville: Thomas Nelson, 2009.

Swindoll, Charles R. *Swindoll's New Testament Insights: Insights on 1 & 2 Peter.* Grand Rapids: Zondervan, 2010.

Swindoll, Charles R. *Swindoll's New Testament Insights: Insights on 1 & 2 Timothy, Titus.* Grand Rapids: Zondervan, 2010.

Swindoll, Charles R. *Swindoll's New Testament Insights: Insights on Revelation.* Grand Rapids: Zondervan, 2011.

Walvoord, John F. and Roy B. Zuck. *The Bible Knowledge Commentary: An Exposition of the Scriptures by Dallas Seminary Faculty.* Old Testament ed. Wheaton, Ill.: Victor Books, 1986.

ABOUT THE WRITERS

John Adair

Th.M., Ph.D., Dallas Theological Seminary

John received his bachelor's degree from Criswell College and his master of theology degree from Dallas Theological Seminary, where he also completed his Ph.D. in Historical Theology. He serves as a writer in the Creative Ministries Department of Insight for Living. John, his wife, Laura, and their three children reside in Frisco, Texas.

Jim Craft

M.A., English, Mississippi College

Jim received his master of arts degree in English from Mississippi College and is currently pursuing a certificate of biblical and theological studies at Dallas Theological Seminary. Jim has served in the Creative Ministries Department at Insight for Living since 2005, where he has the privilege of reading and editing the biblically illumined works of Chuck Swindoll and the Insight for Living team. Jim and his wife, Amber, live in Dallas, Texas.

Malia Rodriguez

Th.M., Dallas Theological Seminary

Malia received her master of theology degree in Systematic Theology from Dallas Theological Seminary. She now serves as a writer in the Creative Ministries Department of Insight for Living, where she is able to merge her love of theology with her gift for words. Malia and her husband, Matt, who is also a graduate of Dallas Theological Seminary, live in the Dallas area with their son.

Wayne Stiles

Th.M., D.Min., Dallas Theological Seminary

Wayne received his master of theology in Pastoral Ministries and doctor of ministry in Biblical Geography from Dallas Theological Seminary. In 2005, after serving in the pastorate for fourteen years, Wayne joined the staff at Insight for Living, where he leads and labors alongside a team of writers, editors, and pastors as the executive vice president and chief content officer. Wayne and his wife, Cathy, live in Aubrey, Texas, and have two daughters in college.

ORDERING INFORMATION

If you would like to order additional copies of *Famous Last Words* or other Insight for Living Ministries resources, please contact the office that serves you.

United States

Insight for Living Ministries
Post Office Box 5000
Frisco, Texas 75034-0055
USA
1-800-772-8888
(Monday through Friday, 7:00 a.m.–
    7:00 p.m. central time)
www.insight.org
www.insightworld.org

Canada

Insight for Living Canada
PO Box 8 Stn A
Abbotsford BC V2T 6Z4
CANADA
1-800-663-7639
www.insightforliving.ca

Australia, New Zealand, and South Pacific

Insight for Living Australia
Post Office Box 443
Boronia, VIC 3155
AUSTRALIA
1300 467 444
www.insight.asn.au

Guatemala

Apartado Postal 1L
Agencia: Aguilar Batres
01011, Guatemala
GUATEMALA
(502) 4769-7509
infogt@visionparavivir.org

United Kingdom and Europe

Insight for Living United
  Kingdom
PO Box 553
Dorking
RH4 9EU
UNITED KINGDOM
0800 787 9364
www.insightforliving.org.uk

Other International Locations

International constituents may
contact the U.S. office through
our Web site
(www.insightworld.org),
mail queries, or by calling
+1-972-473-5136.